MODERN TIMES

GW00729985

Bismarck, the Kaiser and Germany

Titles in this series

WORLD WAR ONE
FRANCO AND THE SPANISH CIVIL WAR
ROOSEVELT AND THE UNITED STATES
HITLER AND GERMANY
MUSSOLINI AND ITALY
THE MAKING OF THE WELFARE STATE
MODERN CHINA
MODERN RUSSIA
MODERN JAPAN
WORLD WAR TWO
WESTERN EUROPE AFTER HITLER
THE LEAGUE OF NATIONS AND UNO
MODERN AFRICA 1870–1970
BISMARCK, THE KAISER AND GERMANY
THE MODERN COMMONWEALTH

The Making of Modern Germany
W. Schenk

These filmstrips deal with the key periods
in the evolution of Germany as a nation.
Contemporary prints, photographs, original
maps and pictographs.

Single frame

The Revolution of 1848
0 7056 0408 X

The Rise of Bismarck
0 7056 0414 4

Imperial Germany
0 7056 0460 8

The Rise of Hitler
0 7056 0461 6

Anna-Maria Goodman

MODERN TIMES

Bismarck, the Kaiser and Germany

B. J. Elliott
UNIVERSITY OF STIRLING

LONGMAN

LONGMAN GROUP LIMITED
Longman House, Burnt Mill, Harlow,
Essex CM20 2JE, England
and Associated Companies throughout the World.

First published 1972
Sixth impression 1983

ISBN 0 582 20423 2

Printed in Hong Kong by
Yu Luen Offset Printing Factory Ltd.

Acknowledgements

The author and publisher are grateful to the Radio Times Hulton Picture Library
and Staatsbibliothek, Berlin for permission to reproduce the photographic material
in this book.
  R.T.H.P.L. pp 6, 14, 25, 28, 31, 34, 44/5, 48, 50, 63, 77, 83, 85, 95, 99, 101, 114,
118, 123, 131, 133, 138, 142, 147, 150 and 153.
  St. B. pp xi, 4, 9 (*left* and *right*), 10, 11, 12, 15, 18, 19, 21, 23, 26, 36, 37, 39, 42,
46, 49, 57, 59, 60/1, 70, 73, 81, 87, 90, 92, 105, 107 and 145.

The maps on pages 51 and 139 are redrawn from H. Holborn *Germany 1840–1945*,
Eyre & Spottiswoode, and on page 2 from W. Carr *A History of Germany*, Edward
Arnold.

Preface

In the twentieth century the name of Germany has become, amongst some people, synonymous with war. Admittedly Germany's geographical position has meant that it has been the traditional enemy of the Slavs, especially the Russians, and, until 1870, the victim of French military power. The links between Britons and Germans were, by contrast, mainly happy ones until 1904, if only through common hostility to France. The royal blood of Britain and Germany frequently intermingled. The husband of Queen Victoria was a German and her grandson William became the Kaiser. There was frequent talk of a military alliance and not for some years after 1900 did a conflict begin to appear probable.

Although parliamentary democracy has been established in (West) Germany only since 1949 it would be wrong to suppose that before that the German people have always suffered dictatorship in dumb misery. One has only to remember the names of Martin Luther and Karl Marx to appreciate that Germany has long been a breeding-ground of protest and original thought.

A little more than a hundred years ago Germany did not exist except as a geographical expression. Yet in half a century the thirty-eight states of the German Confederation were welded into the world's greatest military power and second greatest industrial producer. The principal architect of this transformation was Prince Otto von Bismarck, succeeded, less ably, by Kaiser William II.

In the following pages I have tried to illustrate the lives of these two men and the part they played in this momentous period of German and European history.

Without the researches of many historians, some of whose works are included under 'Further Reading' (p. 161), this book could not have been written. I gratefully acknowledge their labours. My thanks also go to Mrs V. M. Mosedale for an efficient production of the typescript.   B. J. ELLIOTT

Contents

Contents

Time Chart

Prologue

The New Empire

Since before dawn thousands of officers and men of the Prussian and other German armies laying siege to Paris, had been converging on the great palace at Versailles, former home of the French royal family, which lies 20 kilometres to the south-west of the capital. Led by drum and pipe bands and standard-bearers of the 1st battalion of each of sixty chosen regiments they streamed in along roads turned to mud by the cold, wintry rain. Soon the three great avenues leading to the palace were filled with marching men and officers in carriages and on horseback. The assembly point was the vast palace courtyard, the *Cour Des Ministres*, in which stands the equestrian statue of its royal founder, Louis XIV. By mid-morning the courtyard presented a colourful spectacle as the representatives of the armies of the German states gathered to acclaim their new Emperor.

At 10.45 Crown Prince Frederick of Prussia arrived quietly by carriage. Passing through the lines of troops he drew up in the *Cour Royale*, alighted and entered the palace. At the top of the first staircase he entered the *Salle du Sacre*, dominated by three huge portraits of Napoleon I. He passed on through the *Salles des Gardes de la Reine*, so called because three Swiss guards died here defending Queen Marie Antoinette against the Paris mob in 1789, through the *Antichambre de la Reine* and entered the *Galerie des Glaces* (Hall of Mirrors). The Hall is of enormous proportions, 73 metres in length, 10 metres wide and over 13 metres in height. Along the west wall are seventeen large windows overlooking the magnificent park and Grand Canal. Facing these are a similar number of mirrors of equal size from which the Hall derives its name. On the domed ceiling, designed by Charles Le Brun and completed in 1682, are depicted the conquests of Louis XIV. On this cold January day of 1871 it was France herself which was the victim of the conquering armies of the Prussian-led German states.

The generals and colonels of these armies, warmed by numerous fires burning in the great Hall, had gathered around a platform erected against the north wall. On the platform stood an altar, bare apart from two candles and a crucifix. Eight Lutheran clergy stood in attendance. Above the altar hung the colourful standards of the sixty regiments represented at the ceremony.

Soon after midday a hush fell upon the officers and nobles assembled in the Hall. Drums rolled, the choir began to sing and the great doors opened. Surrounded by a bevy of princes, dukes and army commanders, King William I of Prussia entered. He walked slowly across to the platform, bowed to the clergy and took his place at the top of the steps. A short religious

William I

service was then conducted by the court preacher, Roggé. In his sermon he warned the French of the wrath to come if they did not surrender at once. The service ended with the singing of *Nun danket alle Gott* (Now thank we all our God). The king, sometimes trembling, replied with an address of welcome. Then all eyes turned to the huge, pale man wearing the blue uniform and tall boots of the cuirassiers who stood a little apart from the nobility surrounding the king. This was Otto Eduard Leopold von Bismarck, Minister-President (prime minister) of Prussia, whose skilful diplomacy had made this momentous occasion possible. Stepping forward to the foot of the platform Bismarck, in a surprisingly low voice, read out the proclamation:

'We, William by the grace of God, King of Prussia, and after the German princes and free cities have unanimously appealed to us to renew the imperial dignity, which has been in abeyance for more than sixty years . . . hereby inform you that we regard it as our duty to the whole fatherland to respond to this summons of the allied German princes and free cities and to assume the German imperial title. May God grant to us and to our successors to the Imperial Crown that we may be defenders of the German Empire at all times not in martial conquests but in the works of peace, in the sphere of national prosperity, freedom and civilization.'

Grand Duke Frederick of Baden, William's son-in-law, then called out 'Long live his Imperial and Royal Majesty, Kaiser William!' Immediately a great cheer arose from the assembly, helmets were flung in the air, swords waved and men pushed forward to congratulate the new Emperor.

Two days after the proclamation of the new Empire (20 January 1871) *The Times* of London remarked shrewdly: 'Thus begins the new political life of Germany and, whatever may betide, a remarkable period in the world's history is about to be displayed before us.'

1 The Young Bismarck

Germany before Bismarck

As the proclamation speech had noted, only sixty-five years before the foundation of the New Empire, the German people had been subjects of another much older imperial crown – that of the Holy Roman Empire. The long existence of this empire had been a main reason why there was no one united German state before 1871. Within the boundaries of Germany, in 1800, there were well over 300 separate political states with a total population of 24 million. The largest of these states, with nearly 10 million inhabitants, was the Kingdom of Prussia, ruled over by Frederick William II. Bavaria was the second largest with 3 million inhabitants. The remainder, including ninety-seven Rhineland states with a combined population of 1·3 million, ranged down in size to Hirrlingen with 819 subjects. The rulers of these states were not only kings and princes but dukes, margraves, archbishops, abbots, imperial knights and the eight electors who chose the Holy Roman Emperors. There were also fifty-one Free Cities such as Hamburg and Cologne, each ruled in most cases by a powerful committee of lawyers, merchants and members of leading families.

This ancient Empire was politically weak. The Austrian house of Hapsburg which wore the imperial crown had too many troubles outside the Empire to be able to rule firmly. The 300 or so petty princes jealously guarded their power and privileges. Naturally economic life in Germany was also held back. Most agricultural workers were serfs bound to the soil and often forbidden to work in industry. Transport facilities were very primitive, and goods crossing Germany had to pay crippling duties at each frontier. In her intellectual and cultural life Germany, once called a 'land of poets and thinkers', could claim to lead Europe. In 1800 there were twenty-six universities in the Holy Roman Empire. England had two.

Against the opposition of the princes, the movement for the reform and modernization of Germany could not hope to succeed. The Holy Roman Empire was finally destroyed by the

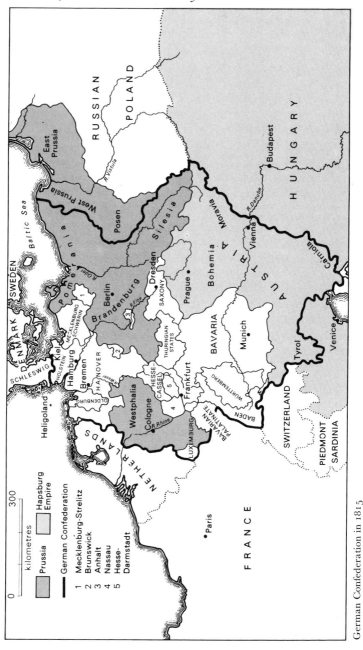

German Confederation in 1815

French Emperor, Napoleon I. Twice he defeated the Austrians in battle and then ordered the frontiers of Germany to be redrawn. Only thirty sovereign German states remained outside the Rhineland which Napoleon himself took over. Then after a third defeat Francis II of Austria announced the end of the Holy Roman Empire.

In 1806 at Jena Napoleon also destroyed the armies of Prussia which was then reduced to one-third of its former size. This massive defeat made the Prussians realise how out-of-date was their state. Important reforms were begun. The peasants were freed and nobles allowed to engage in trade and industry. The army, the civil service and local government were all thoroughly modernized. The educational system was overhauled and expanded.

Prussia was thus able to play an important part in defeating Napoleon at Leipzig (1813) and Waterloo (1815). It became once more a powerful and respected state, rivalling Austria for the leadership of Germany. Because of their rivalry neither power would agree to a single united German state in which the other might be dominant. After Napoleon's final defeat in 1815 the thirty-eight states of Germany were formed into a loose grouping called the German Confederation. These states were still almost completely independent as had been the 300 or more before 1800. They met in an assembly called the Federal Diet, but it was a body without power. Nevertheless, a considerable advance had been made on the chaos of the Holy Roman Empire.

In the manor house at Schönhausen some 90 kilometres west of Berlin a Prussian nobleman named Ferdinand von Bismarck was little concerned with plans to reshape Germany or the oncoming clash of British, Prussian and French armies at Waterloo. He was busy preparing a notice to be placed in the local paper announcing the arrival of his fourth child, Otto.

> I have the honour to announce to my friends that yesterday my wife was safely delivered of a son and I excuse them from offering congratulations.

Schönhausen   FERDINAND VON BISMARCK
2 April 1815

3

The Bismarcks of Brandenburg[1]

Otto Eduard Leopold von Bismarck was born, in April 1815, into an ancient family of the Mark of Brandenburg. The first Bismarck, Herbert, had settled in Stendal in the thirteenth century. His great-grandson, Claus, had been raised to the nobility in 1345 and granted the castle of Burgstall as a reward for his services to the Margrave of Brandenburg. Two hundred years later the family was given the great house at Schönhausen in exchange for Burgstall. The Bismarcks were renowned soldiers. It was said that between the Religious Wars of the sixteenth century and the defeat of Napoleon every generation of Bismarcks 'had drawn the sword against the French'. Three of Otto's uncles and one of his cousins fought Napoleon in the War of Liberation and his father was a cavalry captain in the 1790s. Other branches of the family from southern Germany fought in the French armies in Russia and at Leipzig.

The Junker (noble, landowning) class, to which the Bismarck family belonged, formed the backbone of the Prussian civil service and army. Junkers were usually well-off but not extravagantly rich. They worked hard on their estates rearing sheep and cattle and growing wheat and root crops. They spent little

[1] Most places mentioned in this chapter can be found on the map on p. 5.

Schönhausen

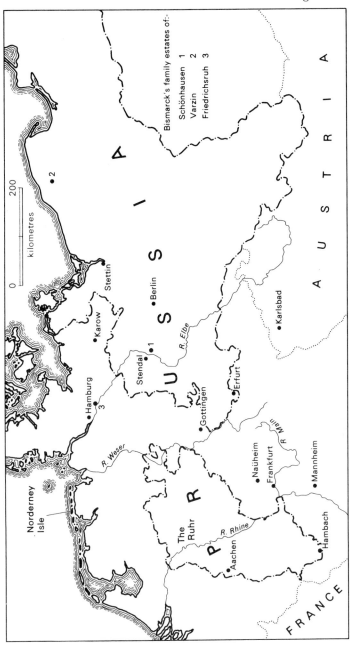

Bismarck's family estates of:-

Schönhausen 1
Varzin 2
Friedrichsruh 3

200

kilometres

0

AUSTRIA

Karlsbad

Erfurt

R. Elbe

Berlin

Stendal

Göttingen

Gottingen

Stettin

Karow

Hamburg

R. Weser

R. Main

Nauheim

Frankfurt

Mannheim

Norderney
Isle

The
Ruhr

R. Rhine

Aachen

Hambach

FRANCE

PRUSSIA

Bismarck's Germany

time in Berlin. Hunting, shooting and visiting each other's houses were their main amusements. Employment in the service of the state provided a valuable extra income and in return for this and a guarantee of their privileges, the Junkers gave the king absolute loyalty. Naturally they opposed any reforms which might threaten this position. They supported serfdom believing that 'our country places will become hell if we have

Wilhelmine, Bismarck's mother

free peasants as our neighbours'. Nevertheless the Junkers paid dearly for their privileges. No less than sixty-four members of the von Kleist family laid down their lives in the service of Frederick the Great during the Seven Years War (1756–63).

Otto's father, the youngest of four brothers, had retired from the army at the age of twenty-three so that he could tend his estates at Schönhausen. The king was angry with him, deprived him of his rank of captain and forbade him to wear his uniform. Ferdinand von Bismarck was a pleasant, good-humoured man. In 1806, when he was thirty-five, he married the sixteen-year-old daughter of the secretary of the Prussian Cabinet. Her name was Wilhelmine Mencken. Unlike her husband, Wilhelmine was extremely clever and ambitious for her children. She gave

6

them encouragement but little love. Otto disliked his mother but admired his father: 'He was the clever, sophisticated son of a clever, sophisticated mother masquerading all his life as his heavy, earthy father.'[1]

Life was not easy for Ferdinand and his young bride. Of the six children born of their marriage only three, Bernhard (b. 1810), Otto (b. 1815) and Malwine (b. 1827), survived. On one occasion the family had to flee from Schönhausen to escape from a band of French soldiers who did considerable damage to the house. However, when Otto was a year old the family moved to Pomerania, where his father had inherited the family estates at Kniephof and Kulz. These estates, some 175 kilometres to the north-east of Berlin, lay in a land of thick woods, wide heaths and rich meadows. It was here that young Otto spent his childhood and developed a love of the countryside which remained with him all his life. 'I just don't like the stink of civilization in big cities,' he said in later years; 'I feel best in greased boots deep in the forest where I hear nothing but the woodpecker.'

The Student of Law

When Otto reached the age of seven his mother sent him to boarding school in Berlin 'in order to break his aristocratic pride'. She chose the Plamann school, which was run according to the ideas of Turnvater Jahn. The aim of this school was to turn out sturdy young Prussians devoted to their country and ready to save it from another defeat and occupation by the French. Life at the Plamann school was very hard.

The boarders were awoken at 5.30 a.m. with a 'rapier thrust', and until 9.30 p.m. their lives were filled with prayer, study, games, fencing, gardening and gymnastics. 'Elastic meat and parsnips' with dry bread was a typical meal. Young Otto suffered greatly from homesickness, made worse by his mother's excuses for not letting him come home during the summer holidays. He disliked the hard life but nevertheless soon proved himself a strong swimmer, a skilful fencer and a natural leader in games. His school report for 1825–6 showed him to be a competent worker in all subjects, except history, but his natural vigour led him to try to finish his work too quickly.

[1] A. Taylor, *Bismarck the Man and the Statesman.*

At the age of twelve he was transferred to the Friedrich Wilhelm Gymnasium in Berlin where he spent five years. He lodged with his elder brother Bernhard, who was a university student. The chief subject at the Gymnasium was Latin but the young Bismarck also learnt to speak English and French so fluently that he later gained the praise of both Disraeli and Louis-Napoleon. He grew tall and slim, with a thick crop of reddish-blond hair and, by the age of fifteen, was beginning to attract the attention of young ladies both in Berlin and on his family estates. In addition to his skill at swimming and fencing he became a deadly shot with both rifle and pistols. It was said that he could blow the head off a duck at 100 metres. Like most young noblemen he was a keen horseman and showed complete disregard for his own safety, although suffering many falls and several broken ribs. While a pupil at the Gymnasium he was confirmed by the famous preacher Pastor Schleiermacher, who told him: 'Whatever you do, do it with all your heart and as from the Lord.' It made a great impression on him.

In 1832, having passed the necessary examination, Bismarck joined the 1,600 students at the Georgia Augusta University of Göttingen in Hanover. The fact that he chose a Hanoverian, and not a Prussian, university shows that Bismarck wanted to make a complete break with his severe Prussian upbringing. It was a very good choice. Göttingen had an excellent reputation and amongst its tutors were the famed collectors of fairy tales, the brothers Grimm. Bismarck, a law student, did not take advantage of the opportunities offered and quickly became notorious for his eccentric appearance and wild behaviour.

'He came strutting down the street followed by a score of shrieking children. Anyone not a citizen of Göttingen would have taken him for an escaped lunatic. He wore the usual beer-cap in flaming crimson and gold, a chaotic dressing-gown – without collar or buttons, enormously wide trousers, and boots with iron spurs and heels. His shirt collar was doubled over his shoulders and his hair, worn long in the Göttingen fashion of the time, fell loosely about his ears and neck. Strapped about his waist was a leather girdle in which were two huge horse-pistols, as well as a long basket-hilted sword, the duelling schlager of the university student.

'The attempt of this slim youth to raise a moustache was not

Otto – schoolboy and student

convincing. His blond scraggly hair topped a face covered with freckles, a face distinguished by a pair of piercing eyes. From the tip of his nose to the edge of his right ear extended an impressive scar, grotesque relic of a recent duel. To complete the effect he had shaved off one of his eyebrows. On his right forefinger he wore an enormous seal ring and in one hand brandished an oaken cudgel. In the other he held a small memorandum book.'[1]

Duelling, although illegal, was the favourite sport amongst students at Göttingen. The students belonged to clubs called fraternities – Bismarck was a member of the Hanoverian – and met their opponents from other clubs at the 'Kaiser' inn outside the town. The aim was to draw blood, almost invariably from the face, with a slash from their razor-edged but blunt-ended swords. Duelling scars were worn proudly by the students as a badge of courage. As a swordsman Bismarck was without equal and earned the nickname 'Achilles the Unwoundable'.

[1] Snyder, *The Blood and Iron Chancellor*.

9

A student duel

During his three terms at Göttingen University he fought twenty-five duels and drew blood from every opponent. He was in fact wounded once himself when his opponent's sword broke. The resulting cheek wound required fourteen stitches. When not duelling Bismarck could usually be found drinking in a beer-house, but rarely learning in a lecture-room. The professors and lecturers so bored him that after a year he transferred to the University of Berlin. Early in 1835 he acquired the help of a private tutor and, with little difficulty, passed his final examinations for a degree in law.

The Civil Servant

When he had finished his education, Bismarck, as a Junker, could enter one of two professions – the Army or the civil service. Having no taste for military discipline he chose the latter and obtained an unpaid post as *Auskultator* (legal examiner) in the Prussian judicial service. He performed his duties at the Berlin Municipal Court very conscientiously. On one occasion he shouted at a difficult witness: 'Take care or I'll have you kicked out.' The judge gently warned Bismarck. 'Herr Auskultator, the kicking out is my business,' he said. The witness continued to be difficult and in exasperation Bismarck again lost his temper: 'Take care,' he roared, 'or I'll have the judge kick you out.'

Berlin in 1830

Life was not all work for the young examiner, who was now lodging with his brother Bernhard in Behrenstrasse. As a member of an ancient noble family he was able to attend the highest social gatherings. It was at one of these that he first met Prince William whom he was to proclaim the German Emperor more than thirty-five years later. The prince looked at the tall, strapping figure of Bismarck and suggested he would do well in the Army. Bismarck replied that his chances of promotion would be poor. 'From what I hear', remarked the prince with foresight, 'your promotion chances in the legal profession are no better.'

After a year in Berlin, Bismarck in fact left the legal service. He applied for, and obtained, a post as Referendary (administrative assistant) in the Rhineland city of Aachen (Aix-la-Chapelle). Aachen had belonged to Prussia only since 1815 and offered a very different life to that which Bismarck had known in Berlin and on the family estates.

It was a colourful, cosmopolitan watering-place, particularly popular with the English. Bismarck was able to mix freely with the international set. He took the customary stroll in the Kurpark, attended the theatre regularly and lost far more than he could afford at the gaming-tables, adding to the debts he had accumulated since Göttingen. It was hardly surprising that he should have fallen in love twice whilst in such romantic surroundings. Both young ladies were English. The first, Laura Russell, was granddaughter of the Duke of Cleveland. It seems that the Duke was more impressed by Bismarck than was Laura. A few months later, however, he 'went overboard' for Isabella Lorraine, the daughter of a Lancashire clergyman. Bismarck left his job and followed Isabella and her family all over Europe. Eventually she married a wealthy, one-armed colonel of fifty. Utterly depressed, Bismarck went on a disastrous gambling spree before returning to Aachen. He found his work unbearable and resigned his post. 'The Prussian official', he wrote some years later, 'is like a member of an orchestra, but I want to play only the music which I myself like or no music at all.' This statement revealed the key to his character – the born leader who would accept nothing but his own leadership.

After a brief period of farming, followed by some administrative work in Berlin, Bismarck joined the *Gardejäger* (Sharpshooters of the Guard) to fulfil his obligation of one year's military service. Bismarck had done his best to avoid this duty but

Gardejäger

his requests to be excused had been turned down. He did, however, manage to obtain a posting to Stettin which was much closer to his home and his sick mother than Berlin. Wilhelmine died on 1 January 1839 and it was decided that the family estates in Pomerania should be administered by Otto and Bernhard whilst his father should live at Schönhausen with twelve-year-old Malwine. Thus Otto von Bismarck returned for eight years to the life he claimed he liked best; that of squire and farmer.

The Squire

As an important landowner Bismarck was both policeman and judge in his own little domain. The family estates needed considerable improvements and the work occupied much of his time. In spite of his claims in later life he does not seem to have been happy to remain a country squire all his life. In many ways he behaved as he had in his student days. He drank vast quantities of beer and champagne and enjoyed playing practical jokes on friends and relatives. Once he released some young foxes in the drawing-room of his female cousins. He had a habit of awakening guests by firing a pistol at the ceiling above their heads and showering them with plaster.

'The mad Junker', as he became known locally, roamed the countryside at all hours mounted on his large brown horse, Caleb. Sometimes he travelled further afield. In 1842 he landed at Hull, was entertained by cavalry officers at York Barracks and visited Scarborough, Edinburgh and the Lancashire cotton towns. He found the British Sunday unbearably dull and was once told off by a stranger for whistling in the street. He considered joining the British army in India but decided not to as, 'the Indians had never done him any harm'. His travels also took him to France, Switzerland, Italy and the island of Nordeney. In 1844 he returned to the civil service, but finding this even more boring than farming left after a fortnight.

Bismarck, in his late twenties, was a fine-looking man. His tall frame was broadening out, his hair was close-cropped and he sported a trim beard. Women were fascinated by him and Bismarck was not slow to return their interest. In 1843 he met Maria von Thadden, the daughter of a neighbouring landowner and fell deeply in love with her. Maria was engaged to,

Johanna, Bismarck's wife

and eventually married, Bismarck's schoolfriend, Moritz von Blanckenburg, but through Maria he met Johanna von Puttkamer. All these three belonged to a strict religious group called the Pietists. Bismarck, who had rejected all religion since his schooldays, was impressed by the peace and confidence which religion gave to his new friends. Late in 1846 an epidemic illness swept northern Germany for which no cure was known. On 11 November Maria von Thadden, only twenty-six years of age, fell victim to the disease and died. Bismarck, still secretly in love with her, was heartbroken, but he was tremendously impressed by the strength of her religious faith throughout her fatal illness.

He also knew that Maria had long hoped that he would marry Johanna von Puttkamer. Johanna lacked Maria's radiant beauty, being slightly built with jet black hair and large dark eyes. She was quiet and reserved and said to be very musical. Bismarck made up his mind to marry her. But with the reputation he had acquired as a wild, irreligious tearaway, he was unlikely to find favour with the von Puttkamers. A month or so after Maria's death Bismarck wrote a long letter to Johanna's father in which he frankly admitted his lack of faith since boyhood. In the previous four years, he went on, his association with the Pietists had shown him the emptiness of his life; his religious faith had returned and he hoped he was now fit to ask

Berlin–Potsdam railway, 1838

for Johanna's hand in marriage.[1] The letter was successful and on 28 June 1847 Otto von Bismarck and Johanna von Puttkamer were married. They went to Venice for their honeymoon. Whilst there seems little doubt that Bismarck was truly reconverted to Christianity at this time, events in Prussia were developing which were to have a much greater effect on his life and eventually on the history of Germany and Europe.

By the late 1840s railway building was in progress in most parts of Europe. Prussia felt the need to build a line from Berlin to the remote province of East Prussia. To pay for this line the state had to raise a public loan. To gain approval for this loan, King Frederick William IV called together representatives of all the provinces of Prussia to a United Diet. The representatives were not popularly elected as are members of modern parliaments or assemblies. They consisted of chosen members of the nobility, members of the middle classes from the towns, and members of the peasantry. A few weeks after the assembling of the United Diet in Berlin one of the deputies representing the nobility was taken ill. Although busy with preparations for his marriage Bismarck agreed to take the place of the sick member. In this casual manner Bismarck found his true vocation and almost without break was to remain in politics for the next forty-three years.

[1] Snyder, *The Blood and Iron Chancellor*, pp. 61–4.

2 The Making of a Statesman

Germany 1815–48

Between the birth of Bismarck in 1815 and his entry into politics in 1847 Germany continued the slow movement begun in 1789, towards national unity and away from the feudal, agricultural type of society. To most people living at the time this movement was not obvious. On the contrary the settlement of 1815, masterminded by Metternich, tried to put the clock back to the eighteenth century. Petty princes, in some cases with records of tyranny and oppression, were welcomed back by hysterical crowds. Thus the middle classes who had gained in power and influence during the Napoleonic period were thrust down again. They were powerless to prevent the corruption, injustices and inequalities which returned in full force. For example, in some states the best seats in theatres were always reserved for the nobility.

Progressive Germans looked hopefully to Prussia, which had given the lead in modernization and reform from 1807 and enjoyed equality with Austria at the peace-making. Under popular pressure Frederick William III had, in 1815, promised to establish an elected assembly. He soon came to regret his promise. He was surrounded by generals and landed nobility who hated reform and were frightened by noisy, but usually harmless, student demonstrations. Frederick William III therefore began to co-operate with Metternich to suppress nationalism and revolution in Germany. In 1819 they joined the representatives of eight other German states to sign the Karlsbad Decrees. These decrees imposed a strict censorship on newspapers, a close supervision upon schools and universities and a sharp watch upon revolutionary groups. Thus in 1819 Prussia (and many other German states) turned their backs on Britain and France, where liberal and democratic ideas were gaining ground. Prussia joined the eastern powers – Russia, Austria and Turkey – in which backward-looking emperors denied their subjects not only the right to elect representatives and governments but also many basic freedoms. Metternich's ideas were accepted in Germany and for nearly forty years Prussia took second place to Austria in German affairs.

Under the threat of the Karlsbad Decrees Germany remained quiet for a decade. In 1832, however, thousands of reformers, including refugees from the recent Polish revolution, met at Hambach in the southern Rhineland. In a noisy demonstration speakers called for greater personal freedom, some demanding the abolition of the monarchy in German states and the establishment of a German republic. Thoroughly alarmed, the authorities carried out many arrests, but most reformers escaped to America, Britain, France and Switzerland. Laws were passed forbidding popular meetings. Thus Germany escaped political revolution for the time being.

Economically, as well as politically, Germany appeared to be making little headway after 1815. The textile industry relied heavily on domestic workers; factories were very small and the use of steam power extremely limited until after 1850. The iron industry was also old-fashioned. The use of coal for smelting instead of charcoal developed only slowly because the vast coalfields of the Ruhr were untapped until the late 1830s. The firm of Krupp, which provided much of Germany's military strength in the twentieth century, employed only 122 men in 1846. Industrial concerns wishing to use machinery and increase their output were hampered by a great shortage of money.

Behind this poor condition of German industry in the early nineteenth century the future of its economic strength was being laid. The educational reforms of the early nineteenth century were already beginning to show results. In 1840 Dr John Bowring, sent out from Britain to examine German economic life, reported on the high standards of training and achievement amongst scientists. Bowring also noticed that in Germany 'metals were most successfully wrought and worked'. Steel castings from the Krupp works attracted much attention at the Great Exhibition in London in 1851. Of greater immediate importance to the development of Germany were the abolition of internal customs duties between the states and the development of transport facilities.

Trade in Germany was strangled by the succession of customs

duties payable on goods, but in 1818 Prussia had taken the first important step forward towards the establishment of a German customs union (Zollverein). This was the Tariff Law drawn up by the Finance Minister Karl Maassen which allowed raw materials to enter duty free and manufactured articles at a duty of 10 per cent of their value. Tropical products such as sugar were charged 20–30 per cent. Several small neighbouring territories joined the Prussian system during the next few years. In southern Germany after ten years talking Bavaria and Württemberg formed a customs union. Several smaller states in central Germany, alarmed by what seemed the end to their customs revenues, formed the Middle German Customs Union. The members of the Union aimed to prevent any tariff changes but one by one they dropped away to join Prussia. Bavaria and Württemburg also joined and in 1834 the German customs union covered an area of over 400,000 square kilometres with a population of over 23 million. Most states did not join the Zollverein with the intention of trying to create a united Germany. Their main hope was to increase their revenues and in this they were successful. Customs duties rose by 88 per cent in the first nine years. Manufacturers and traders, freed from crippling tariffs, expanded their businesses, to the benefit of most sections of the community.

Prussia also took the lead in improving communications with-

Early German Steamship

out which economic life would remain stunted. Between 1817 and 1828 4,400 kilometres of good roads were built. Charges made on the great rivers of Germany – the Rhine, the Elbe and the Weser – were reduced and steamships were in regular service by 1830. The greatest improvement in German industrial and political development came as a result of railway building. By 1840 the Prussian government was involved in building railways, a decision which brought Bismarck into politics (p. 15). By 1850 across the German Confederation three lines from north to south and three from east to west had been built. By 1860 Prussia alone had 5,600 kilometres of track on her territories.

Heavy industry – coal, iron, steel, engineering, timber and brickmaking – grew enormously during the railway boom. Not only did railway building use up the products of these industries. Through the opening of new lines, mines and factories in distant regions were able to send their products to all parts of Germany and Europe.

Thus by the 1840s the German States were rapidly uniting in transport, trading and industry, the natural result of which would be political unity. It was again to Prussia that nationally-minded Germans looked hopefully. In 1840 the opponent of change, Frederick William III, died and was succeeded by his son, Frederick William IV. The new king was a very cultured,

Frederick William IV

intelligent and charming man, who often spoke proudly of the 'German nation'. Frederick William's reign did not keep its early promise. At heart he was not a liberal and he was opposed to those who wanted more political freedom and to those who were working for a united Germany. Thus when he called the United Diet in 1847 to seek approval for the East Prussian railway loan it became immediately clear that there was a vast gulf between Frederick William IV and the growing band of politically conscious Prussians. 'Prussia', said the king in his opening speech to the Diet, 'was made great by the sword of war and internal discipline and must continue to be ruled by its king'. The Lower House of the Diet, faced by the king's opposition to reform, refused to agree to the railway loan. Although the Diet achieved very little it had established that citizens had a right to meet and discuss freely the affairs of the kingdom.

Berlin 1848

One deputy who certainly did not support the liberal call for political reforms was Otto von Bismarck. When making speeches he appeared ill at ease and tended to stammer. But through his fierce attacks on the reformers, Bismarck quickly became the chief spokesman of the Junkers and the king's supporters. He was a staunch defender of the monarchy, denying that the people had any right to elect a national assembly.

However, when it refused the East Prussian railway loan, the United Diet was dismissed. Bismarck married, took a leisurely honeymoon and did not return to Germany until harvest time. Early in the New Year (1848) Europe erupted into a series of national revolutions. These uprisings were protests against the crushing power of foreign rule, tyrannical governments, privileged nobility and harsh factory owners.

The year of revolutions began in Sicily and Naples. By the end of February, the barricades had gone up in the streets of Paris and King Louis Philippe had been forced to abdicate. In Germany the first sign of unrest was a mass meeting at Mannheim in the south Rhineland state of Baden. Here and elsewhere in Germany the princes quickly gave way to the reformers. In Austria Metternich's long rule came to an end and he fled to England. Disturbed by this news from Vienna,

Frederick William IV of Prussia promised to work for a united Germany. He agreed that the first move in this direction should be the summoning of a German national parliament at Frankfurt in the Rhineland. When these promises were announced in Berlin joyful crowds surrounded the royal palace. Unfortunately, in the confusion two shots were fired into the air by troops guarding the palace and the mood of the crowd changed dramatically. Believing that the king was betraying them the crowds rioted and scores of barricades were flung up across the streets. Although the army quickly set about restoring order the king unexpectedly ordered the troops to withdraw from the capital while he remained there unprotected.

Bismarck was visiting the estate of a friend at Karow when he heard the news from Berlin. He was enraged by the treatment of the king and thought of gathering a peasant army to rescue him. Instead he hurried to Army headquarters at Potsdam where he found the soldiers eager for action but the generals

Berlin barricades, 1848

unwilling to move without authority from above. Bismarck then tried to see the king but was refused permission. Frustrated and seething with anger he plotted counter-revolution.

His plan was that, since Frederick William IV had lost freedom of action, he should be replaced by his nephew as king. Bismarck hurried to see the young man's mother, Princess Augusta, to gain her consent to the plan. The princess, realizing that Bismarck had for the time being lost his ability to think clearly, flatly rejected the scheme. The result was a lifelong feud between the two.

Meanwhile the plan for a German national parliament had got under way. At the end of March politicians gathered at Frankfurt and with the approval of the Federal Diet (p. 3) decided to hold elections on 1 May for a parliament which would draw up a political constitution for all Germany. The 585 elected members of the Frankfurt Parliament duly met at St Paul's Church in that city on 18 May 1848. It was one of the most distinguished gatherings in German history, 'more than 100 professors, more than 200 learned jurists, writers, clergymen, doctors, burgomasters, senior civil servants, manufacturers, bankers, landowners, even a few master craftsmen and small tenant farmers – but not a single worker. There were . . . worthies from provincial towns and universally beloved and famous poets, orators, historians and politicians.'

In Berlin also a new liberal regime took power in May 1848. Obviously at such a time the arch-enemy of reform, Otto von Bismarck, had no chance of securing a seat in the National Assembly. He returned to Schönhausen, where he sat around the house smoking heavily and refusing to talk. Bismarck's restless energy soon led him back into political activity. He became a member of a Junker Party which tried to overthrow the liberal government. By the mid-summer of 1848 things were going badly for the revolutionaries all over Europe. In December General Wrangel entered Berlin and the liberal-dominated Assembly and government were overthrown. Frederick William IV did not abolish universal male suffrage but replaced it by an indirect system which made the votes of nobles worth much more than those of ordinary people. When elections for the new National Assembly were held Bismarck gained a narrow victory and took his seat in February 1849.

The Frankfurt Parliament

Meanwhile the Frankfurt Parliament had been patiently laying the foundations for a united Germany. It decided that an Emperor (Kaiser) should be head of the German state, that he should be elected by the Assembly and afterwards the title would become inherited. On 28th March 1849 Frederick William IV of Prussia was elected Emperor of Germany and a deputation travelled to Berlin to offer him the crown. The king, failing completely to sense the feelings of the German people, refused the crown by election. He would only accept it if it were offered by all the German princes. Bismarck, by then holding a seat in the Prussian Assembly, bitterly attacked the Frankfurt parliamentarians for trying to unite Germany by popular elections. When Frederick William IV refused the Imperial Crown the German revolution of 1848, and with it the Frankfurt Parliament, came to an end. The spirit of revolution and the desire for German unity could not be killed. The strong political feelings in Germany were too great for this.

Frederick William did, however, agree to the creation of an assembly of northern German states at Erfurt. But the Austrians, supported by Russia, forced him to give up this idea, much to the disgust of most Prussians. One Prussian who supported Frederick William and his government was Otto von Bismarck. He argued that a war with Austria and Russia over the establishment of the Erfurt Assembly would have been stupid. 'Only two things mattered for Prussia,' he said, 'the avoidance of an alliance with democracy and the securing of equality with Austria.'

As a result of this stern defence of the government, Bismarck was given his first post with the diplomatic service. In 1851 he became Prussian minister at the revived Federal Diet at Frankfurt. Apart from a spell in Vienna he held the post for eight years.

Frankfurt

It was most unusual for a deputy of the National Assembly to be appointed to a diplomatic post. Probably few cared that a highly conservative Junker should represent conservative Prussia in the outdated Federal Diet. As the sternest defender of the government Bismarck was thought to be the least likely to oppose and annoy the Austrians at Frankfurt. Nothing proved to be further from the truth.

Travelling alone to Frankfurt, Bismarck took rooms in the home of a wealthy Rhinelander who did not like Prussians. After his request for a bell in his rooms had been ignored, Bismarck took to calling the servants with a pistol shot. The bell was soon installed. His first courtesy call was upon the President of the German Confederation, Count Thun. It was a warm day. When Bismarck entered the count's office he found him seated at his desk in his shirtsleeves, smoking. Asked to wait Bismarck showed his impatience by taking out a cigar and asking Thun for a light. He then removed his own jacket remarking, 'Yes, it is warm.' By the customs of the times both Bismarck's actions were extremely bad-mannered. Bismarck was in fact demonstrating that Prussia was to be considered Austria's equal. In the Federal Diet Bismarck behaved with equal firmness. If the Austrians suggested a plan of action, Bismarck insisted that it be debated line by line. 'When Austria hitches a horse in front,' he wrote, 'we hitch one behind.'

Merely to obstruct Austria was not enough for a man of

Bismarck's temperament. He wanted Prussia to become the major power in Germany, a situation which could only be achieved if Austria were totally excluded from German affairs. Bismarck also realized that to drive Austria out Prussia must first control northern Germany. Only then would Prussia have sufficient military and political strength to overcome Austria. The smaller states began to feel nervous of Prussia and they supported Austria in most debates. Bismarck continued to attack Austria in the Federal Diet which resulted in his fighting a pistol duel with one deputy. Alexander I of Russia became so worried about the quarrels between his friends that he sent a special ambassador, Prince Gortschakov, to try to bring Austria and Prussia together.

Vienna, 1864

In 1852 Bismarck found himself en route to his 'enemy's' capital – Vienna – as Prussian Ambassador. The appointment was for a few months only as the permanent ambassador was ill. He was well received and had the opportunity of meeting the young emperor, Francis Joseph, who was to rule Austria until 1916.

Bismarck returned to Frankfurt during the Crimean War and in 1855 he visited Paris for the World Fair. Here he met for the first time the Emperor Napoleon III and struck up a friendly relationship with the man against whom he was to go to war in 1870. Bismarck's stay at Frankfurt was drawing to an end. In 1858 Frederick William IV became insane and his

25

brother Prince William was appointed Regent of Prussia. William, a steady, mediocre but strong-willed man, was devoted to the army. His greatest ambition was to become commander-in-chief of the armies of the German Confederation. Whilst having a great respect for Bismarck, William disliked both his policies and his behaviour at Frankfurt. He decided that Bismarck must be replaced and early in 1859 William appointed him as Prussian Ambassador to Russia.

St Petersburg

Bismarck was ambassador at the Tsar's court, in the city built by Peter the Great, from April 1859 to April 1862. He certainly did not regard his new appointment as promotion. The journey

St. Petersburg

from Berlin took five days as the railway link had not then been completed. In wintertime the journey involved long hours on horseback through deep snow and freezing temperatures. In St Petersburg (now called Leningrad) Bismarck was almost cut off from German and European politics. During his stay he suffered not only from isolation but poor health, including bouts of rheumatism. He also suffered financial hardship on a salary of £3,750 per annum. Most ambassadors received about four times as much with which to meet the heavy expenses of an embassy.

Within weeks of his arrival in Russia war again broke out in Europe. This time the dispute was between France and Austria over lands in northern Italy. Russia had promised France to remain neutral but Prussia was in a difficult position. If she supported Austria, Prussia would lose the opportunity to become the major power in Germany. If she helped France to defeat Austria, Prussia might then have to face Napoleon III singlehanded. Bismarck had no doubt who the principal enemy was – Austria. 'The present situation has once again put the great prize in the lottery-box for us', he wrote to Prince William, 'if we only allow Austria's war against France to eat quite deeply into her substance. Then let us march southwards with our whole army with the boundary posts in the soldier's knapsacks and drive them into the ground either at Lake Constance or where protestantism ceases to prevail.'

Unfortunately, from Bismarck's point of view, a quick peace-making between France and Austria ended his plan to extend the Prussian frontier to Switzerland. Bismarck was soon engaged in his own personal war for survival. While hunting in Sweden he struck his leg violently against a rock. By the time he had returned to St Petersburg he was suffering severe pain and unwisely he allowed himself to be treated by a quack calling himself 'Doctor' Walz. The treatment consisted of putting a plaster, evidently containing some corrosive substance, on the back of the knee. Bismarck was soon in agony, and the plaster had to be scraped away leaving a huge raw wound and destroying a vein. As soon as he was able, Bismarck left by sea for treatment in Germany. On the ship a Russian surgeon, Pirogov, inspected the leg and recommended amputation. Bismarck refused this drastic measure and following treatment at Berlin and in the medical baths at Naüheim, began to recover. Then inflammation of the lungs set in and his death was awaited hourly. He survived and after a ten-month absence returned to his duties at St Petersburg in May 1861.

Bismarck was held in high regard in Russia, particularly by the Tsar Alexander II and Prince Gortschakov. In turn he developed a respect for Russia, for its enormous size and potential power, which remained with him throughout his life. As Chancellor of the German Empire, Bismarck always tried to keep friendly relations with Russia. Nevertheless in 1861 he was not expecting to remain as ambassador to Russia for long and was relieved when in the spring of 1862 he was recalled to Berlin.

Paris

In 1861 Frederick William IV died and Prince William ascended the throne of Prussia as William I. Prussia was in the grip of a political crisis. The National Assembly had a large liberal majority but the conservative William insisted on appointing ministers who supported his own point of view. The National Assembly refused to support William's army reforms. Many important Prussians realized that only Otto von Bismarck had the strength and determination to lead a government which could overcome the Assembly. William I, most reluctant to call upon Bismarck, sent him instead to Paris as Prussian ambassador. During his three months in his new post Bismarck spent very little time in Paris. He had one long conversation with Napoleon III after which each decided to try to mislead the other about their future plans. He visited London where he talked to Disraeli, leader of the Opposition. 'When the army has been brought to such a state as to command respect,' said Bismarck seeing himself in power, 'then I shall take the first opportunity to declare war on Austria, burst asunder the German Confederation, bring the middle and smaller states into subjection and give Germany national unity under the leadership of Prussia.' This was a remarkable prophecy. It impressed Disraeli who observed: 'Take heed of that man, he means what he says.'

Napoleon III

From London Bismarck moved on 4 August 1862 to the French Atlantic coast resort of Biarritz. He took a room at the Hotel de l'Europe and was shortly joined by Prince Orlov, the Russian ambassador to Belgium and his wife Katharine. Bismarck, now forty-seven, fell in love with the beautiful twenty-two-year-old Katharine. He toured the south of France with the Russian couple, reminding himself of the time he had pursued Isabella Lorraine a quarter of a century before.

For Bismarck this last youthful adventure was soon to be over, as power and responsibility were placed upon him. On 12 September a letter arrived from the Prussian Minister of War, Albrecht von Roon, warning him that he could expect to be appointed head of the government very shortly. At Avignon station Bismarck said goodbye to the Orlovs as they left for Geneva and he caught the Paris train. In Paris he read German newspapers which reported the king's deadlock with the National Assembly over army reforms. On the 16th he received a telegram from the Foreign Minister urging him to come to Berlin.

On the 18th von Roon sent him the famous message 'Periculum in Mora. Depêchez-vous.' (Delay is dangerous. Hurry.)

Bismarck immediately hurried to Berlin by train and was taken to Babelsberg Castle just outside the capital where William I was living. Two days before William had been discussing his possible abdication with Crown Prince Frederick. Now he was meeting Bismarck, who, he had said several times, was beyond control and could never head the Prussian Government. He told Bismarck that he could find no minister who would carry out his wishes for army reform in the face of opposition by the Assembly. Bismarck told the king that his abilities 'such as they are, are at your Majesty's disposal', and that he would prefer to be executed 'rather than leave your Majesty in the lurch in your battle with Parliament'. William was astonished by this vow of loyalty.

The following day he signed the order appointing Bismarck President of the Ministerial Council (prime minister) of Prussia.

He was to remain in power for twenty-seven years.

3 The Unification of Germany

Minister-President of Prussia

Few men, on becoming head of government, have appeared less fitted than Bismarck was in 1862. His experience in administration, more than twenty years previously, had been slight. As a diplomat at Frankfurt he had devoted his energies to annoying the Austrians. At St Petersburg he had lived a lonely existence, ill and short of money. In Prussia his new appointment was extremely unpopular. One political leader wrote: 'Bismarck, that is to say: government without budget, rule by the sword in home affairs and war in foreign affairs. I consider him the most dangerous Minister for Prussia's liberty and happiness.' Many foreign newspapers also wrote unfavourably about the appointment.

Bismarck was not at all upset by this reception. First, he formed a cabinet of ministers whom he could trust. Then he began to dismiss civil servants who opposed his policies. His first important task was to settle the dispute, in the king's favour, between William and the National Assembly. William believed that the Prussian army was small, badly trained and ill-equipped. He had decided therefore, to create an additional forty-nine regiments which would almost double the size of the army. He also planned to re-equip the army with the most up-to-date weapons. To achieve this William had found that it would be necessary to increase compulsory military service from two to three years. The military budget would also have to be increased by £1·5 million. In 1861 the National Assembly rejected this increase. Bismarck had to make sure that William's military reforms would be carried out.

At his first appearance before the National Assembly, Bismarck held up an olive leaf as a gesture of peace. 'The government has always stretched out its hand for a settlement' he declared. Then becoming careless and over-confident in his speech, he warned the Assembly that 'the position of Germany will be determined by its power . . . not through speeches and majority decisions are the great questions of the day decided, but through *iron and blood.*'

He then settled the argument about the military budget by withdrawing it. In future, he announced, he would manage without a budget. He was able to do this because the government had an adequate income from taxation and from state-owned mines, forests, railways and posts. Some Liberal deputies suggested that the people should refuse to pay taxes. Bismarck warned that he had 200,000 soldiers ready to help the tax collectors.

Bismarck's solution to the budget dispute made him even more unpopular. The National Assembly declared his actions illegal. The War Minister von Roon condemned his *iron and blood* speech. Bismarck reacted by persuading the king to ban newspapers which were hostile to the government. Although the ban lasted only a few months it was bitterly opposed by Crown Prince Frederick and his English wife Princess Victoria

Crown Prince Frederick and family

(daughter of Queen Victoria). Frederick felt that Bismarck was making the people hostile to the Prussian monarchy. Thus after only a year in office Bismarck was thoroughly disliked, sometimes to the point of hatred, by the people, by the majority of politicians and by most of the royal family.

War with Denmark

Bismarck cared nothing for cheap popularity. When deciding on a course of action, he considered only what would be best for Prussia. Thus in 1863, when the Polish subjects of the Russian Tsar rose in rebellion, Bismarck offered his support in crushing the outbreak. In making this offer, which annoyed Britain and France, he nevertheless felt that he had to warn Prussia's own Polish subjects against disloyalty. Also he thought that he might reduce the threat of an alliance between Russia and France. Later in the year he sabotaged a German princes' conference organized by Austria. By threatening to resign, a technique often to be repeated, Bismarck persuaded William I not to attend. Without Prussia the conference was meaningless.

In his attitude to the Polish rebellion and the princes' conference, Bismarck was simply preventing what would be harmful to Prussia. Very soon he was given the opportunity to direct events himself. Henceforth, he worked to unite all the German states under Prussian leadership; the very thing he had fought to prevent in 1848.

Bismarck's opportunity to direct events came with the death of King Fredrick of Denmark in November 1863. At this time Denmark was much larger than it is today, stretching as far south as Hamburg. The southern part included the territories of Schleswig and Holstein which were ruled by the Danish king with the title of Duke. The subjects of Schleswig were mixed Danish and German but those of Holstein overwhelmingly German. Holstein was a member of the German Confederation.

In 1848 the German inhabitants of Schleswig and Holstein, helped by Prussia, had risen in rebellion. However, the Great Powers of Europe, Britain, France, Russia and Austria, intervened to prevent any change in the situation. Unfortunately, the Danish king had no children and females were barred from becoming rulers in the Duchies. It was inevitable that when the king died there would be trouble, because there were rival claimants to the Duchies. The Great Powers named the Danish Prince, Christian of Glucksburg, while most Germans supported the Duke of Augustenburg.

Unlike the majority of Germans, Bismarck had no intention of supporting Augustenburg. He intended to make the Duchies part of Prussia but he knew that the Great Powers would oppose him. Britain was the most outspoken in defence of Denmark but Bismarck was sure she would not act alone. Russia would not help Britain because of growing enmity between the two in many parts of the world. This left only France and Austria. Bismarck made sure that Napoleon III would not interfere by making vague promises of Rhineland territories to him. Finally he rounded off his plans for the conquest of Schleswig and Holstein by persuading Austria to *join* the invasion and share the spoils. The Austro-Prussian treaty was signed on 16 January 1864, and the two armies attacked on 1 February.

The Danes, although reinforced by volunteers from Sweden

Bismarck's Wars 1864–71

33

Danish defences, 1864

and Norway, were greatly outnumbered. However, hoping for early British help, they decided to fight. Bismarck was pleased because this meant that he would secure the Duchies by right of conquest, although he did not make public his secret plans of seizure until 3 February. The Austro-Prussian forces had first to storm the Danewerk, a line of forts across the neck of the Jutland Peninsula. Unexpectedly the Danes abandoned their defences and retired to Duppel. The invaders marched northwards through the Duchies. One detachment of Prussians entered Denmark and captured Kölding on 18 February. Britain mumbled more threats but in April Duppel was stormed and a truce called. A conference was held in London but Britain, France and Russia could not agree to stand up against Prussia and Austria. The Danes refused to accept any of the suggestions from the conference and fighting began again in June.

The Prussian army, which had done little to distinguish itself, carried out a landing on the Isle of Alsen. Realizing that the Prussians would soon overrun all Denmark, the Danes surrendered. A peace treaty was signed in Vienna in October 1864. King Christian of Denmark surrendered his rights over Schleswig, Holstein and the territory of Lauenburg to Prussia and Austria. Bismarck had won his first victory in international affairs.

War with Austria

Bismarck soon let the Austrians know that he wanted the former Duchies to become part of Prussia. Austria of course could never agree to the humiliation of handing over her conquests. Bismarck therefore began to plan war between Austria and Prussia. After her defeat Austria would then be excluded from German affairs. The growing quarrel was temporarily patched up at Gastein in August 1865. Prussia took over the government of Schleswig and purchased Lauenburg for £1 million. Austria administered Holstein.

Bismarck however was still resolved on war. Although certain that neither Britain nor Russia would interfere in a Austro-Prussian war, he was worried about France's position.

Napoleon III was known for interfering in the affairs of others. Bismarck had to be sure that he would not try to imitate his famous uncle, Napoleon I, by marching into Germany. In October 1865 Bismarck travelled to the French resort of Biarritz to visit Napoleon, who was staying with the Empress at the Hotel Villa Eugenie. Bismarck also nursed the hope of meeting his former love Kathi Orlov. However, a cholera scare had led the Russian princess to visit Devon instead.

It is not known what Bismarck and Napoleon said to each other except that neither made any definite promises. Bismarck probably made vague references to Belgium, Luxembourg and the Saar, hoping to whet Napoleon's appetite. Napoleon for his part had no objection to Austria and Prussia fighting a long exhausting war. Confident of French neutrality Bismarck returned to Berlin to continue his war of nerves on Austria. Early in 1866 he turned his attention to Italy which was trying to drive the Austrians out of Venetia. With the permission of William I Bismarck signed an alliance with Italy whereby the latter would join Prussia in any war which broke out between April and July 1866.

Bismarck now had to annoy Austria sufficiently so that she would act rashly and give him the excuse to declare war. With both countries arming themselves for the coming struggle Austria suddenly tried to win the support of the smaller German princes. On 1 June 1866 Austria asked that the Federal Diet (i.e. the princes) should settle the future of Schleswig and Holstein. Prussia replied by marching into Holstein. Three days later Prussia put forward plans for a united Germany from which Austria would be excluded. Austria called upon the princes to join her against Prussia. On 12 June Austria and Prussia broke off relations and four days later Prussia invaded Saxony, Hanover and Hesse-Cassel, which had sided with Austria. Neither Saxony nor Hesse offered resistance but at Langensalza on 28 June, the Hanoverians were driven from the field.

Austrian artillery at Sadowa

The decisive battle of the war, between the Austrian and Prussian forces, was fought on 3 July 1866. The site of this battle lies today in Czechoslovakia about 100 kilometres east of Prague, between the village of Sadowa and the fortress of Königgratz. The battle is known by either of these last two names. The Austrians with the larger population, numerous allies, and high military reputation were widely regarded as favourites. On this day their army of 215,000 were slightly outnumbered by Prussia's 221,000. The Prussian army had a brilliant commander in Count Helmuth von Möltke and was equipped with the new needle-gun. This weapon was effective only up to 600 yards because it lacked a gas-tight breech but its rate of fire was four times as high as the weapons of the Austrians. The Austrians, however, had a fine artillery force which pinned down the first Prussian advance. Then, with the fortunate arrival of a Prussian army under Crown Prince Frederick, von Moltke was able to spring his trap on the Austrians, attacking from both flanks and the front. At the end of the day 40,000 Austrians lay dead on the field and about

Prussian cavalry at Sadowa

half this number were taken prisoner. Prussia lost 10,000 dead.

Bismarck was on horseback for thirteen hours on the day of the battle. Unmoved by the wholesale slaughter around him, he was distressed to come upon a horse badly mutilated by a shell. As he was unarmed he could not put it out of its misery. Most of his time was spent at the king's side keeping him out of danger. With shells landing all around Bismarck pleaded in the name of the Prussian people that the king should move to a safer spot. 'Well, then, Bismarck,' said the king, 'let us ride a little,' and began to amble away. 'I felt very uneasy about him,' wrote Bismarck later, 'and so edging up with my dark chestnut to the king's mare, I gave her a good kick from behind with the point of my boot; she made a bound forward, and the king looked round in astonishment. I think he saw what I had done, but he said nothing.'

The North German Confederation

Although the Austrians were completely beaten, Bismarck could not afford to relax. Firstly he feared a Franco-Bavarian alliance followed by an attack on Prussia. He was also worried about Russia which, having helped to create the new Germany in 1815, was very upset by Bismarck's control over Central Europe. Finally, Bismarck had to restrain the Prussian generals who, supported by the king, wished to destroy Austrian power entirely and march through Vienna in triumph. 'We shall need Austria's strength in future for ourselves,' pleaded Bismarck. Crown Prince Frederick, a liberal intelligent man agreed with Bismarck but it was only when the latter threatened suicide, that the king changed his mind. An armistice was signed at Nikolsburg on 23 July.

To prevent the French joining the war Bismarck reluctantly agreed that Napoleon III should mediate between Austria and Prussia in discussing a peace treaty. This was signed at Prague exactly one month after the armistice. It was agreed that Prussia should have several smaller German territories. With twenty-one other states lying north of the River Main, Prussia formed the North German Confederation. The new Confederation was to have a specially drawn up constitution (see pp. 50–3), and its own parliament (Reichstag). Napoleon, fearful of Prussia's future power, insisted the four major states lying south of the Main, Bavaria, Württemberg, Baden and Hesse, were to remain independent of Prussia. Austria which had 10 million German-speaking inhabitants was shut out of Germany for ever (except during Hitler's rule, 1938–45). The Austrians were also obliged to surrender the Italian province of Venetia in spite of having defeated the Italians on land (Custozza) and at sea (off Lissa).

Bismarck returned to Berlin in triumph with the king, General von Moltke and a procession of 200 captured Austrian guns. A new Diet had been elected on the day of Konniggratz-Sadowa. The Conservatives, who supported Bismarck and the

Varzin

king in their army expansion programme, gained the largest number of seats – 142 out of 354 – whilst the Liberals dropped to 85. The new Diet encouraged by popular support forgave Bismarck, legalising his earlier budgets. A grateful nation promoted him Major-General and awarded him £60,000. With the money he bought a run-down estate at Varzin in Pomerania complete with house, which his wife Johanna called a 'crooked monstrosity'. Bismarck, however, always stayed there for a few weeks each year.

In his treatment of Austria's former allies Bismarck himself showed no generosity. Bavaria was fined 30 million guilders (£3 million), Hesse 3 million, Württemberg 6 million and Saxony 8 million. Upon the free city of Frankfurt a crippling fine of 25 million guilders was imposed, with a penalty of 1 million for each day it remained unpaid. The *burgomeister* (Lord Mayor) hanged himself.

The Quarrel with France

After her defeat by Prussia in 1866 Austria was weak and demoralized. In a bid to strengthen his multinational empire, Francis-Joseph II agreed to the setting up of the dual monarchy of Austria-Hungary. This meant that he took the title of King

39

of Hungary and a separate parliament and government was established at Budapest. Foreign, military and financial policies were united and there were no customs posts between the two countries. Because she was now kept out of Germany and Italy in 1866 the new Austro-Hungarian Empire had only one part of Europe in which it could actively interfere. This was the Balkan peninsula, inhabited mainly by Slav peoples who, busily throwing off Turkish rule, had no wish to become subjects of the Austrians. The Slavs looked to the Russians, who were also Slavs, for protection. Russia, which longed to get control of the warm-water sea route through the Bosphorus (see map on p. 68) thus became Austria's rival in the Balkans. Both Russia and Austria looked to Prussia for support but Bismarck had no wish to choose one and make an enemy of the other. In the late 1860s he was more concerned with the difficult problem of France.

Napoleon III was becoming increasingly worried about the growing strength of Prussia and Bismarck's ability to outwit him. In 1867 Napoleon tried to take over Luxembourg, which was ruled as a Grand Duchy by the King of Holland and garrisoned by Prussian troops. Bismarck was not opposed to Napoleon buying Luxembourg, but the Diet of the newly founded North German Confederation utterly opposed its transfer. Not only did Napoleon fail to get Luxembourg, but in the same year his unhappy attempt to turn Mexico into a French satellite state ended disastrously. Napoleon and his ministers were determined to prevent any further failures of their foreign plans. In particular they were not prepared to allow Prussia to unite with the four South German states thus creating a giant German state. 'If Bismarck draws the South German States into the North German Confederation,' said Napoleon, 'our guns will go off by themselves.' In his determination to contain Prussia, Napoleon tried to make alliances with Austria, Italy and Russia but without success.

Bismarck, noticing the hostility to Prussia amongst the South German states, did not believe that German unification would be possible in less than twenty-five years unless there was war with France. Such a war appeared less likely when early in 1870 a new French government took office. It accepted that one day Germany would be united and announced that it would not intervene provided that Prussia did not try to conquer the South Germans.

War with France

In September 1868 the Queen of Spain, Isabella, was driven off her throne and into exile, along with the whole Bourbon family. General Prim, the Minister of War, took charge of the country while serious efforts were made to find a new monarch from among the royal houses of Europe. Bismarck decided that an anti-French king on the throne of Spain would be an additional worry for Napoleon. The man Bismarck decided to support for the vacant throne was a German Catholic prince, a distant relative of King William. The prince's name was Leopold von Hohenzollern-Sigmaringen, and he was also brother-in-law of the king of Portugal. To support Leopold's claim Bismarck sent a secret envoy to Spain with £50,000 to bribe the Cortes (Spanish parliament). William I was most unenthusiastic about the whole affair, and Leopold himself could not be persuaded to accept the idea until June 1870.

Bismarck hoped that the election of Leopold could be carried out secretly in July before the French could stop it. However, the news leaked out, reaching Paris on 3 July. By this time, France had a more nationalist foreign minister, the Duc de Gramont, who was being pushed by many important Frenchmen to take a firm stand against Prussia. On 6 July de Gramont made a bitter speech against Prussia calling upon the Hohenzollerns to give up their bid for the Spanish throne.

Leopold promptly obeyed the French demand, a move approved not only by William but also by most of the great powers. Bismarck was annoyed and humiliated but refused to resign. Napoleon, his cabinet and the French press were overjoyed by their victory over Prussia. Unfortunately Napoleon, excited by this, made a mistake which gave Bismarck the opportunity to save his position. Napoleon ordered his ambassador to Prussia, Benedetti, to see King William, and get him to promise not only that Leopold would withdraw his bid for the throne but that he would never renew it.

William was staying at the health spa of Ems at this time and met Benedetti in the Park during a morning stroll on 13 July. William listened to Benedetti's demands, accepted the first but

Count von Moltke

firmly refused to make any promises for the future. Before lunch he sent a telegram to Bismarck who was in Berlin describing the morning's events. The telegram arrived in the evening while Bismarck was dining with his old friends from the war office, von Roon and von Moltke. Its arrival added to the air of gloom hanging over the diners. Then with a sudden burst of inspiration, Bismarck took up his pen and began to reword it. When he had finished it appeared that Benedetti had behaved so badly in public that the king had refused to see him again. The French ambassador had been 'shown the door' like a persistent street hawker. Bismarck had transformed a simple message into a thunderbolt which would soon destroy Napoleon III.[1]

By late evening the edited telegram had appeared in special editions of the Berlin papers. Before dawn it had been tele-

[1] See Richter, *Bismarck*, p. 171.

graphed to Prussian embassies throughout Europe with instructions to submit it to the various governments. When King William saw it he said with a shudder, 'This is war'. When the French learnt that it had been sent across Europe they realized that Bismarck was winning another diplomatic victory.

France fell into the trap set by Bismarck. On 14 July mobilization began, the extra costs being voted by the National Assembly. On the 19th war was declared. The rest of Europe remained neutral although, for different reasons, King Victor Emmanuel of Italy and the Emperor Francis-Joseph of Austria would have liked to support France. Thus France had to stand alone with an army of less than 300,000 of whom only 202,000 were ready by 31 July to meet the main Prussian advance. Prussia and her South German allies could muster 450,000, of whom 309,000 were concentrated in two wings along the Rhine between Mainz and Strasbourg (see map, p. 33).

The outbreak of war united all Germans with patriotic enthusiasm. Württemberg, Hesse and Baden immediately declared their support for Prussia; Bavaria did the same after some hesitation. The basis was laid for the unity of north and south Germany. Bismarck, highly pleased by this news, went to war on 31 July. He left Berlin by train, dressed in a blue cavalry overcoat, spiked helmet and thigh-length riding boots. Travelling as far as Mainz on the Rhine, he took up residence in the house of a winemaker, who quickly complained of Bismarck's enormous capacity for food and drink. When the king left for the war front Bismarck shadowed him in a carriage pulled by four brewery horses.

The two armies clashed on 6 August in two separate battles. At Spicheren the Germans drove the French back but suffered 4,500 casualties to the French 2,000. At Worth a much larger engagement took place between 97,000 Germans and 49,000 French. The turning-point came when, to cover their retreat, the French commander ordered his cavalry to charge the Prussians in the village of Morsbronn. The result was a disaster. Prussian riflemen and gunners mowed down the French until one street was completely blocked with the bodies of horses and men. The remainder of the French army then came under heavy artillery fire until resistance collapsed at 4 p.m. Both sides lost around 11,000 men each, and in addition, 9,000

The Prussian advance, 1870

French prisoners were taken. It took French and German doctors three days to bring in all the wounded from where they had fallen.

This battle showed clearly that no longer could cavalrymen stand up to gunfire. It also ended any possibility of a French invasion of Germany. Indeed France now faced invasion herself. At this point Napoleon III lost his nerve and ordered his advance forces, 180,000 men under the command of Marshal Bazaine, to fall back on Metz. This they did in some disorder, hotly pursued by German forces who crossed the river Moselle to the south cutting off Metz from Paris. In trying to restore communications with the capital, the French forces engaged the German army in two fierce battles on 16 and 18 August. After some critical moments, the German forces drove the French back into the fortress of Metz and laid siege to it. Bismarck was deeply distressed to be told of the death of his eldest son, Herbert, and of a serious wound inflicted on his second son, William, at the hands of French cavalry. He rode all night to the battle-front only to find to his relief that Herbert had a slight leg wound and William was unharmed.

By the end of August only one French army was left in the field, under the command of Marshal MacMahon. At first it appeared that MacMahon was moving westwards to make a

stand in front of Paris. Then he changed direction to try to raise the siege of Metz. After some costly clashes with German patrols, he retreated to Sedan. Here he hoped to rest and reorganize. The German army gave him no time and early on 1 September the last and greatest battle of the war began. High on a hill to the south-west of Sedan was a distinguished audience; King William, Bismarck, von Moltke, most of Germany's princes and several international observers, including General Sheridan of the United States Army.

Early in the battle, MacMahon was struck by a shell splinter, but a new commander General de Wimpffen was already on the way. In spite of the terrible battering the French were receiving, Wimpffen refused to allow a retreat. 'We need a victory,' he said, only to be told, 'You will be very lucky, *mon général*, if this evening you even have a retreat.' Eventually an attempt to retreat had to be made and again the cavalry were sacrificed uselessly as at Worth. Repeatedly they charged down the hill towards the mass of Prussian infantry, gaining the admiration of King William and of German officers who allowed the survivors to ride away unharmed. Napoleon III spent the day riding among his troops hoping for a bullet to spare himself the humiliation of surrender. He was unharmed.

That night Bismarck, von Moltke and Wimpffen met to discuss terms. Bismarck persuaded the French to prevent further bloodshed. The following morning Napoleon and 84,000 French troops surrendered. Napoleon and his court were taken to Kassel as prisoners. On 4 September Napoleon was deposed by a revolutionary government in Paris. Much to the surprise of Bismarck and the Prussians the war did not end then and there. When the new French government discovered that Prussia wanted the rich frontier provinces of Alsace-Lorraine it resolved to fight to the end. Bazaine held out in Metz until 27 October. Partisan units attacked German troops, who replied by burning villages and shooting captured irregulars. Paris was besieged, and to speed its collapse Bismarck ordered it to be bombarded. Eventually the city surrendered on 28 January 1871. Peace negotiations at Frankfurt resulted in the French handing over Alsace-Lorraine and paying a fine of £200 million. The cost of the war to Germany was 28,000 dead and over 88,000 wounded.

Meanwhile despite Bavarian doubts and a long quarrel between Bismarck and the king about the latter's future title, preparations for the declaration of the German Empire went ahead (see Prologue). On 18 January 1871, ten days before the French collapse, Bismarck achieved his ambition. Germany was united.

The Prussian entry into Paris

4 The Imperial Chancellor

The Family Man

Bismarck was almost fifty-six years of age when the German Empire was proclaimed, and he became Imperial Chancellor in January 1871. His royal master, now the Kaiser (Emperor) William I, was seventy-four and was to survive to the great age of ninety-one. Bismarck held the post of Imperial Chancellor throughout the reign of William I but was to retire two years later in 1890.

During the years 1864–71 Prussia had won three outstanding military victories and all Germany had been united under her leadership. The architect of these successes was Bismarck. By 1871 his name had become a legend. For nearly twenty years he was without dispute the world's most famous and respected statesman. No less than fourteen towns in the United States were named after him. Bismarck's image was helped by his physical appearance. Although not quite a giant he was very tall and broad, running heavily to fat. He weighed 112 kilogrammes. He had lost most of his hair but made up for this by his luxuriant eyebrows and a magnificent walrus moustache which almost hid his mouth. Yet, curiously for so big and impressive a man, his voice was very high-pitched. For much of his life Bismarck suffered ill-health. His wife, perhaps understandably, called him a 'poor sick chicken'. He had complained of chest troubles since the 1840s and the leg injury suffered in Russia continued to plague him from time to time. He also suffered greatly from toothache, though he refused to see a dentist. More harmful to his health was his gross overweight, brought about by over-eating and drinking. For example, one of his suppers consisted of eight hardboiled eggs followed by several ices. He was once observed in the Reichstag swallowing eighteen glasses of brandy-and-water during one speech. Naturally he suffered from indigestion and sleeplessness and if disturbed at a meal was frequently sick afterwards.

Constant ill-health, caused partly by worry, led him from one doctor to another in search of a cure. Invariably his over-

Bismarck in 1877

bearing manner and great fame prevented their being firm enough with him. In 1883 the situation changed when he consulted Dr Schweninger. Bismarck said he did not like being asked questions so Schweninger told him to go and see a vet: 'He doesn't question his patients.' Bismarck recognized that he had met his match and followed Schweninger's advice. He adopted a special diet of herrings, reduced his drinking and lost 25 kilogrammes in weight. Bismarck then lived in quite good health for most of his remaining fifteen years. Schweninger was rewarded by being made Professor of Medicine at Berlin University.

When not performing public ceremonial duties Bismarck was most careless about his dress. His favourite indoor garment was a dressing-gown, even when receiving foreign diplomats. He wore a black and yellow gown at Frankfurt and at Varzin, his new country home, a grey and violet one. Another strange item he carried in Berlin was an old-fashioned lorgnette. In the country, however, he wore spectacles because he said there was more to see. His house in Berlin, on the Wilhelmstrasse, formerly belonged to Frederick the Great. It was small and cramped, scarcely fitting for the Chancellor of the greatest power in Europe.

'He stayed in these inconvenient quarters for twenty-eight years, always giving visitors the impression he was "camping"

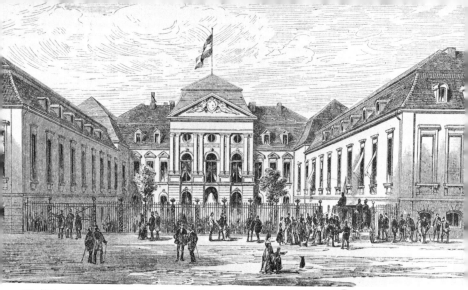

The Palace of the Reich-Chancellor

there. His study was littered with books, bric-à-brac and costly presents from the Tsar. Paintings were piled against the walls. Upstairs some of the carpets were never laid. The kitchen was inadequate for a public man; and the food had to be sent in from a restaurant on the one occasion in the year when Bismarck entertained the diplomatic corps to dinner.'[1]

Bismarck sometimes tried to excuse his simple style of life by pleading poverty. In fact this was quite untrue. He was a large landowner, having been granted a vast estate at Friedrichsruh near Hamburg in 1871 and his lands had been improved. He raised cattle, which were sold to Germany's growing towns. The timber from his extensive forests was sold to coalowners for pitprops, or for conversion to paper. Bismarck himself owned papermills which supplied both the Imperial Post Office and the German railways. Characteristically, he also owned brandy distilleries.

Family life did not, however, offer much comfort. His wife Johanna hated Berlin and spent most of her life in the country, often separated from Bismarck for long periods. Like her husband, Johanna suffered severe ill-health; in her case asthma, which left her thin and very tired. Bismarck's eldest son, Herbert, followed his father into the service of the state. The two men quarrelled violently because Herbert wanted to marry

[1] Taylor, *Bismarck The Man and The Statesman*, p. 87.

49

Bismarck and family, 1893

Princess Elisabeth Carolath who was undergoing divorce. Eventually Bismarck had his way and rewarded Herbert's obedience by promoting him through the diplomatic service to State Secretary for Foreign Affairs. Bismarck's second son, William, also worked in administration but was lazy and became enormously fat. Like his father's, William's health was saved by Dr Schweninger but he was long outlived by his wife Sybille.[1] Bismarck's first grandchildren were provided by his daughter Marie, wife of Count Kuno Rantzau. Bismarck and Johanna spoilt Marie's three boys completely. More grandchildren appeared after Herbert's marriage in 1892.

The German Empire

The constitution (or system of government) of the new German Empire was the handiwork of Bismarck. It was virtually the same system which he had designed for the North German Confederation in 1867. Alterations were made in November 1870 following treaties between Prussia and the South German

[1] Sybille committed suicide in 1945 as Russian troops closed in on Schönhausen. Afterwards they burnt it to the ground.

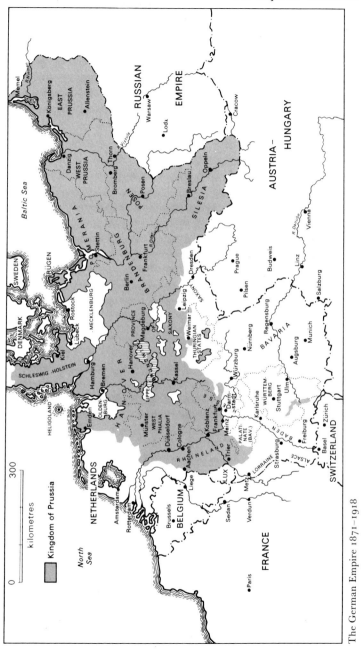

states. The constitution became law on 20 April 1871. In drawing it up Bismarck had been primarily concerned in creating a working relationship between his royal master and himself. Thus the head of the Empire was always to be the King of Prussia. The ancient title of *Kaiser* was adopted to please the Bavarians. The Kaiser alone could appoint or dismiss his chief minister, the Imperial Chancellor, the office which Bismarck held from 1871 till 1890.

Under the new constitution the Kaiser (which effectively meant Bismarck) was in sole charge of foreign affairs. He alone could receive ambassadors, make treaties and alliances and declare war. The Kaiser was commander-in-chief of all the armed forces of Germany's states, but special privileges of command and administration were granted to Württemberg and Bavaria in peace time. The duty of assembling or dismissing the two houses of the National Assembly was also that of the Kaiser. Before a law became effective it had to be signed by both the Kaiser and the Chancellor.

The process of making laws for the German Empire began in the Upper House, the Bundesrat. Representatives in the Bundesrat came from the various states and each state was represented according to its size and power. Thus of the fifty-eight seats, Prussia had seventeen, Bavaria six and Saxony and Württemberg four each. A motion to alter the constitution could be defeated by fourteen votes. This meant that Prussia (of which Bismarck was prime minister) could effectively block any changes. Although Prussia had less than 30 per cent of the seats in the Bundesrat, in practice she was never in danger of being outvoted by a combination of smaller states. The Imperial Chancellor was president of the Bundesrat.

The Lower House, the Reichstag, was a popularly elected assembly. All men over twenty-five years of age had the vote. Until the reign of Kaiser William II (1888–1918) the Reichstag had little opportunity to play an effective role in Germany. Its members were unpaid until 1906, which prevented all but a few working men from gaining seats. In any case working men who stood as candidates could expect most support from Germany's growing cities, yet no provision had been made to provide new seats in these areas of growing population. The Reichstag had no control over the army or foreign affairs. It could refuse to pass budgets, but this method had failed in Prussia in the early 1860s. Few deputies were willing to risk another defeat. The Reichstag could not even cross-examine government ministers (as the British Parliament does) because there were none. Germany had one minister, the Imperial Chancellor, answerable only to the Emperor. The Chancellor in turn appointed departmental heads, 'senior clerks working under the old man's orders'.[1]

If the powers of the Reichstag were limited so also were those of the Imperial administration. For the Empire was not a centralized, unified state as was France for instance. Authority was divided between the central government and the individual states. Only the latter could raise direct taxation. The Imperial Revenue, most of which was spent on the army, came from indirect sources such as customs duties and the profits of the railways and post office. Power was also divided. The Emperor's men controlled the armed forces, foreign affairs and communications. The states ran their own education services and courts of law and dealt with religious matters. Another factor which undermined the unity of the Empire was the presence of large numbers of foreign-speaking (and unwilling) subjects. These were Poles in the east, Frenchmen in the western provinces of Alsace-Lorraine and Danes in the north.

Bismarck and the Catholic Church

Bismarck was only too aware of the delicate balance of the German Empire. It was almost solely due to his skill and diplomacy that the German states had united under one Emperor. For the remainder of his period in office Bismarck was fully occupied in making sure that they remained united. In particular this meant that he was hostile to any forces either inside or outside Germany which seemed to threaten the unity of the Empire.

The first struggle which Bismarck fought on behalf of the Empire was against the Roman Catholic Church. Germany was not the only nation to find itself in conflict with the Pope at this time. The Catholic Church was very conservative and hostile to new ideas. In 1864 the Pope attacked what he called 'progress, liberalism and recent civilization'. This was a period

[1] Carr, *A History of Germany 1815–1945*, p. 138.

of great economic and social change in Europe when the outlook and way of life of millions of men and women were altering. For example in 1859 Charles Darwin published his *Origin of Species* and between 1867 and 1894 the three volumes of Karl Marx's *Das Kapital* were published.

The Papacy itself was in a difficult position at this time. The Italian states were uniting into a single kingdom under Victor Emmanuel. The Pope lost his lands in Central Italy and in 1870 the troops of Victor Emmanuel entered Rome. With nothing left except his Vatican estates the Pope felt that his spiritual freedom was also in danger. Simultaneously at a great conference, the first Vatican Council, it was proclaimed that the Pope could not be guilty of error when making solemn announcements on matters of faith and morals (the doctrine of Infallibility). Some statesmen feared that these facts might lead to a much more militant attitude on the part of Catholics. It was thought that some Popes might try to imitate the Popes of the Middle Ages who issued orders to kings and emperors and passed judgment on domestic quarrels.

Bismarck, born of a stern Lutheran background, was no friend of the Catholic Church, but he was on good terms with the German bishops and had no intention of being other than neutral. Unfortunately for him he was involved in this religious problem through no fault of his own. A number of German Catholics (about 50,000 eventually) refused to accept the Vatican announcement on Papal infallibility. Three German bishops asked the government to dismiss these 'Old Catholics', as they were known, from teaching posts in schools and universities. Bismarck refused. The matter might have rested there but in 1870 a new political party, the Centre, was formed by German Catholics.

The expulsion of Austria, with its large Catholic population, from German affairs in 1866 and control by Protestant Prussia had united Catholics in the political field. By the spring of 1871 the Centre Party had fifty-seven deputies in the Reichstag, making it the second largest party. Moreover the Centre attracted the support of other minority groups, particularly from those deputies who represented foreign-speaking citizens.

Bismarck was very alarmed by the rise of the Centre and its allies. He especially feared an alliance between the party and his old enemies, Austria and France, whose governments supported the Pope. Fearing that the Centre was a very real danger to the security of the Empire Bismarck began his offensive in June 1871 with a series of violent newspaper articles. In July the Catholic section of the Prussian Ministry of Church Affairs and Education was abolished. By August Bismarck had decided to attack not merely the Centre Party but the Catholic Church in Germany itself. In December clergy were forbidden to mention politics while preaching. In March 1872 the Jesuits, the greatest of religious orders, were forbidden to enter schools or to preach. The government were given wide powers which led to the expulsion of most Jesuits from Prussia and later from all Germany.

In 1873 Adalbert Falk, a lawyer who disliked the Catholic Church intensely, was appointed Prussian Minister of Ecclesiastical Affairs. Under Falk Prussia's struggle against the Church reached its full force with publication of the 'May Laws' of 1873. Only men who had studied at German schools and universities and could pass an examination before a state board, could become active priests or ministers. The aim of this was to ensure that priests were loyal to Germany rather than to the Pope. Another law made the state responsible for the discipline of the Church over its members. In 1874 banned priests could be placed under 'house arrest' or even expelled from Germany if they continued to serve their congregations.

The Church responded by passive resistance gaining strength from persecution. By 1876 every Prussian bishop was in prison or in exile. A third of the parishes were without a priest. In 1875 every religious order except the nursing orders had been abolished. Most German Catholics supported their Church's struggle and support for the Centre Party grew. Its votes doubled by 1874 giving it 91 seats, well below the National Liberals' 155, but nearly twice as many as the next party, the Progressives.

By 1876 Bismarck was wearying of the struggle, well aware that the Catholic Church was gaining strength from persecution. Most of the royal family, particularly the liberal Crown Prince Frederick and his English wife Victoria, were hostile to Bismarck's religious persecution. Bismarck realized that the actions of Prussia over the previous five years were doing more to weaken and divide Germany than to strengthen it. With the death of the old Pope, Pius IX, in 1878, Bismarck's opportunity came to end the struggle. The new Pope, Leo XIII, wrote to the Kaiser on the day of his election expressing a wish for better relations. Thus the 'May Laws' were repealed, the clergy returned to their parishes and Falk was 'thrown to the wolves'. Nevertheless many restrictions remained on the Church and the Jesuits were still banned. Even in defeat a statesman as great as Bismarck could salvage something from the wreck of his policy.

Bismarck and the Socialists

The end of the struggle between the Prussian Government and the Catholic Church was merely one part of a dramatic change in Bismarck's policies in 1878–9. In foreign affairs he took a most important step by making a secret alliance with Austria (see p. 71). At home the support of the Centre Party, although limited, was a necessary step towards his most ambitious plan. Bismarck was determined not to rely any longer on the support of the National Liberal Party and at the same time to rid the Empire of what he regarded as the menace of socialism.

The first German Socialist Party had been founded in 1863 by a group of fifteen men meeting in Leipzig. Their leader was Ferdinand Lassalle, the thirty-eight-year-old son of a Jewish merchant. The ill-treatment of Jews in Germany (long before Adolf Hitler) helped to convince Lassalle that revolutionary socialism would mean fairer treatment for all men. Although he studied hard at the Universities of Breslau, Berlin and Paris, Lassalle was more a man of action than a thinker. It was as a man of action that he died, wounded in a duel, barely a year after founding the party. At this time less than 5,000 Germans had joined the Socialists. In 1869, however, Lassalle's followers joined south German Socialist groups led by August Bebel and Wilhelm Liebknecht to form the Social Democratic Labour Party. At an important conference at Gotha in May 1875 the Social Democrats drew up their programme. This condemned private business and wanted the state to take over industry. coalmines and banks. It demanded that all profits should be shared amongst the workers. It called for the removal of social injustices in Germany and believed that workers of all nations

Ferdinand Lasalle

should work to help each other in their fight.

Bismarck was not at first hostile to the Social Democrat Party. In the early days he had had friendly discussions with Lassalle. In any case the party gained only two seats out of 397 in the 1871 elections. Bismarck, the great landowner, did not understand the lives and thoughts of miners and factory workers. It was among these men in the growing industrial cities of Berlin, Essen, Dortmund and Duisburg that Social Democracy began to gain a hold. By 1877 nearly half a million Germans voted Socialist compared with the 120,000 in 1871.

All his life Bismarck feared revolution. He had been born at the end of the wars which stemmed from the French Revolution of 1789. He had been greatly involved in Prussian politics in 1848, the 'year of revolutions'. He had always been completely loyal to the king, when the latter was threatened by the masses or the growing political parties. In 1873 he brought together the Emperors of Germany, Austria and Russia in a League to resist change and revolution (see p. 66). By the late 1870s he was beginning to fear international Socialism as much as he had feared international Catholicism in the early 1870s. How, thought Bismarck, could one be loyal to both Germany and a worldwide movement? In a bid to reduce Socialist influence, Bismarck introduced a Bill into the Reichstag in 1876 which would have given the Government power to control the Press. The Bill was thrown out.

The National Liberal Party had been Bismarck's main ally since 1867. One of their strongest beliefs was in free unrestricted trade between nations. This belief was beginning to embarrass Bismarck for by the mid-1870s the German economy was in difficulties. A growing population and a series of bad harvests forced Germany to import two million tons of cheap Russian wheat. Germany's farmers (of whom Bismarck was one) suffered serious financial losses.

At the same time a slowdown in trade throughout Europe and the USA after 1873 hit Germany's small manufacturers heavily. Many had been in business only a year or two and were forced to close down. To prevent further damage to German economic life Bismarck planned to charge heavy tariffs on imports of food and industrial goods. The National Liberals opposed this partly because the increased customs duties would go to the Imperial Government and therefore weaken the power of the Reichstag.

Bismarck's opportunity to get rid of both the National Liberals and the Socialists came in the summer of 1878. In May a plumber named Hödel fired shots at the eighty-one-year-old Kaiser in Berlin. Bismarck ordered one of his deputies to introduce an anti-Socialist Bill into the Reichstag. It failed to pass. Less than a month later a second attempt was made on the Kaiser's life. This time the assassin, a Dr Karl Nobiling, almost succeeded. William was rushed back to the Royal Palace streaming with blood. Bismarck was strolling through the fields of his estates at Friedrichsruh, exercising his Great Danes, when the news was brought. He stopped in his tracks as an inspiration came to him. He would dissolve the Reichstag and through the Government press attack the National Liberals for disloyalty in refusing to protect William against the Socialists. The fact

Hödel's assassination attack

that Dr Nobiling had no connection with the Socialists did not worry Bismarck. He felt sure the National Liberals would then lose heavily in the elections and the new Reichstag would pass his anti-Socialist laws.

This strategy worked exactly as planned. The National Liberals and Progressives lost forty seats and the Conservatives and their allies gained thirty-seven. An anti-Socialist Bill was laid before the Reichstag. It was opposed by 94 Centrist, 39 Progressives and 9 Social Democrats. The Conservatives supported the Bill and the National Liberals, reeling from their defeat and fearing to risk another election, allowed it through. Socialism was banned in Germany and the Act was extended four times. Not until Bismarck fell from power in 1890 was it repealed. Some 1,500 Socialists were sent to prison and many emigrated to the USA. Newspapers and other publications were banned. Support for Socialist policies nevertheless increased. Votes rose from 437,000 in 1878, to 763,000 in 1887 and in 1890, after Bismarck's fall, rose to nearly 1½ million. By 1912 the Social Democrat Party was the largest in the Reichstag.

As a clever politician, Bismarck realized that he could not defeat socialism solely by force. Therefore he decided to win the workers away from revolutionary socialism by offering them state welfare schemes. As a result of Bismarck's policies Germany became the first state in the world to introduce insurance schemes against the harsh effects of sickness, injury and old age. The first measure, passed in 1883, gave certain free medical treatment and up to thirteen weeks sick pay to 3 million workers and their families. The workers paid two-thirds of the contribution and their employers one-third. A worker who was sick for more than thirteen weeks or permanently disabled was offered protection under the Accident-Insurance Act of 1884. The cost of this was borne entirely by the employers. Seven million agricultural workers were also covered by these Acts in 1886. Finally in 1889 came old age pensions for persons over seventy and disablement pensions for the younger. The cost of this measure was shared by the workers, the employers and the state.

Krupp works in Essen, 1866

The Socialists bitterly opposed Bismarck's 'state-socialism' calling it 'the crumbs off a rich man's table'. Many workers thought the whole programme was a fraud because at the same time their elected representatives could still be banned and locked up. The cost of the scheme which included the 'sticking in of 11 million stamps every Saturday evening' alarmed many people, particularly employers, who could see no immediate benefit in it for them. Germany proved well able to bear the cost in spite of the depression of the late 1870s. During the period of Bismarck's rule developments took place which made Germany a giant among the world's industrial and trading nations.

Economic and Social Developments 1871–90

The foundations of German economic development had been laid before 1870 (see p. 17–19). By that date 17,000 kilometres of

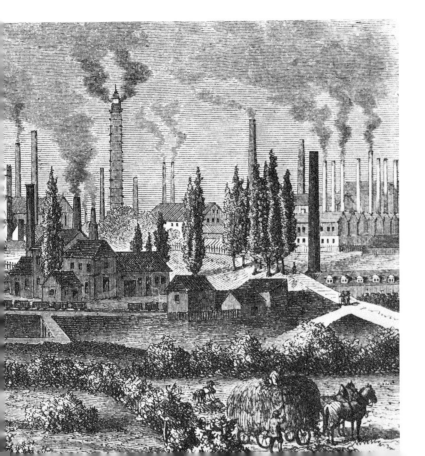

railways had been built and the customs union was almost complete. The development of the great coalfields of the Ruhr and Silesia had been under way for two decades. Iron and steel manufacturers such as Krupp were already famous throughout Europe. But in 1870 Germany was not thought of as an industrial power of the first rank. It was during the Bismarckian era that the enormous expansion of German industries began. Before Bismarck died Britain had become very worried about this powerful new rival for world markets and France had abandoned any hope of single-handed revenge for 1871.

Germany's population continued to grow rapidly until 1904 after which time the birth-rate began to fall. So although a quarter of all children born died in their first year and nearly 2 million persons emigrated the population of Germany increased from 41 million in 1871 to nearly 50 million in 1890. This increasing population provided workers for the growing industries.

Moreover these workers were skilled and educated because the German education system was the finest in the world. By 1869 all Prussian children received eight years compulsory schooling. German universities and technical schools provided the most advanced scientific training in Europe. As a result a constant stream of highly educated recruits went into the science-based industries such as chemicals and electricals, and into banks and commerce. As industries grew so did Germany's cities. During Bismarck's Chancellorship Berlin's population increased from 774,000 to 1,888,000 and Essen's from 100,000 to 290,000. Between 1882 and 1895 employment in agriculture (including families) declined by 700,000 while the population making a living from industry, transport and trade rose by more than 5 million.

After 1870 there was plenty of money available to develop industry. In the 1850s and early 1870s a number of banks were founded whose particular purpose was to attract money for use in industrial development. Often a banker joined the board of directors of a large firm. Here he was able to advise on financial matters such as opening export markets, investing money abroad and agreements, mergers and takeovers in Germany. Once German industry was safe behind high tariffs (1879), mergers and agreements increased rapidly. One type of agreement was the cartel; there were eight cartels in 1875 and ninety in 1885. The purpose of cartels was to limit competition and ensure that each member made a good profit. To stop over-production each member had a quota and was fined if he exceeded it. Cartels saved many firms from foreign competition but they forced up prices and left German industry open to interference by governments.

A large, efficient railway network was the key to German economic expansion. Between 1870 and 1880 the length of track increased by over 80 per cent to a total of 33,800 kilometres. By 1890 it was well over 40,000 kilometres. River and canal transport were also important but railways carried 75 per cent of freight. The bulk of this freight was coal. Between 1870 and 1890 coal production rose from 38 million to 89 million tons. By starting large-scale production relatively late Germany was able to use modern techniques and avoid many earlier mistakes. Coalmines were large, employing an average of 400 men each in the Ruhr in 1880, and growing continuously. The German coal industry had strong and close connections with the iron and steel industry. In fact, many coalmines also yielded iron ore in the early days. Nearly one third of Ger-

German locomotive, 1870

many's coal was used by the iron and steel industry. It was her vast steel industry, second only to the USA, after 1895, which gave Germany her industrial and military might. In 1871 Lorraine, rich in iron ore, was annexed from France. This greatly helped in the growth of steel. From 300,000 tons in 1870 production of steel rose to 2·2 million tons by 1890. Much of this steel was used by Germany's shipbuilding industry. During the 1880s Germany's merchant fleet overtook that of France and most of her 1·5 million tons of shipping was built of steel and powered by steam.

The greatest industrial achievement of the German Empire was the setting up of her chemical and electrical industries which in many fields were world leaders. These industries showed clearly the importance of scientific training and research. Britain led in chemicals in mid-century but her 'coal-tar amateurs scientists were soon out of their depth', unable to understand the difficult scientific processes involved in the chemical industry. Germany was the leading producer of dye-stuffs and plastics partly because she had ample raw materials – salt, potash, iron pyrites and, of course, coal. Electrical development was pioneered by the Americans but Germany proved an able competitor. Werner von Siemens developed the dynamo in 1867 and electric traction in 1879. No electrical workers were listed in the census of 1882 but the following year the great AEG firm was founded. Power stations were built, driven by waste hot gases from the Ruhr blast furnaces. In 1891 the long-distance transmission of electricity was made possible. By the census of 1895 26,000 electrical workers were employed in Germany.

As a growing industrial producer with a rising population Germany's foreign trade also rose dramatically. By 1890 she was buying annually from abroad foodstuffs worth £70 million and raw materials worth £80 million. Her own foreign sales could not pay for these products but, like Britain, Germany had other sources of income. German ships and banks served foreign customers and much freight moving across Europe was carried part of the way on German railways. During Bismarck's time in office about 80 per cent of Germany's foreign trade was with other European countries. Competition with Britain in the great overseas markets was still in the future.

5 World Statesman

The League of Three Emperors

Until 1870 the strongest power in Western Europe had been France, balanced in the east by Austria and, less obviously, Russia. In times of great disturbance Britain was ready also to use her wealth and naval strength to settle affairs. When Bismarck became Chancellor Austria and France were defeated powers. Britain was occupied with the world outside Europe, and Russia was busy with her frontier regions in Central Asia and the Far East. Germany thus found herself the strongest power in Europe, a position which she was to maintain until 1945 in spite of her losses in World War I. The general reaction in Europe to the arrival of this new giant was unfavourable. France was bitterly determined to recover Alsace-Lorraine. Britain feared that Bismarck would soon send his armies marching again – into Switzerland or Holland. Russia suspected that Bismarck would want to take over the Baltic coast provinces where many German settlers lived. Another area where Bismarck was thought to have take-over plans was the German-speaking provinces of Austria.

None of these fears was to have any justification. Bismarck was quite content with the foreign conquests already made. He wanted no more foreign-speaking subjects in the German Empire nor Austrian Catholics either. He had no intention of annoying Russia by speaking out for the Baltic Germans. Nor did he wish to stir up trouble with Britain by building a navy or at first claiming colonial territories. He had used wars to unite Germany but he realized in 1871 that another major war might shatter the German Empire. In particular he realized the danger of a war with two major powers, say France and Russia. Because of its central position Germany was open to attack from two sides and to a sea blockade as well. Bismarck's aim was to keep the peace in Europe although he had no objection to, say, an Anglo-Russian war over India.

It appeared to Bismarck that only one country might threaten the peace of Europe, namely France. Although bitter at losing both her position as the major European power and her provinces of Alsace and Lorraine, it was most unlikely that France would make a single-handed attack. With Italy too weak, and Britain quite unwilling to help, only Russia or Austria appeared as possible partners for France. Bismarck was therefore determined to keep the friendship of the two great eastern empires. In this matter he had, he believed, one major advantage. Germany, Russia and Austria were all states in which power rested firmly with the monarch. France was a Republic with a democratically elected, some would have said revolutionary, government. The Russian Tsar in particular disliked revolutionaries.

Within a few months of the proclamation of the Empire, Bismarck was busy with his plans to isolate France. He was lucky that the foreign ministers of both Austria and Russia, Count Andrassy and Prince Gortschakov, each feared that the other was trying to make an alliance with Germany. Bismarck had no such intentions but he was able to bring the three Emperors together in Berlin in 1872 to show their common friendship. The following year a vague agreement was drawn up, the so-called League of Three Emperors. It was no military alliance, merely an agreement to consult each other on matters of importance. Bismarck made some fuss about defending monarchy against republicanism and socialism but this was mere talk. When Spain became a republic in 1874 Bismarck recognized the new government without consulting Russia or Austria. France was a very different problem. Bismarck wanted France to remain a republic, whereas the Prussian ambassador at Paris, Count Harry von Arnim, favoured a return to monarchy. Bismarck, infuriated by Arnim's disobedience, had him hounded from office and eventually brought to trial. Arnim died in exile.

The League of Three Emperors could not in fact isolate France, whatever Bismarck wished. This was shown beyond doubt in 1875. By this time France had completely recovered from her defeat in 1871, quickly paying off the massive fine inflicted by Prussia. The French government also announced plans to increase the strength of the army by 144 battalions. Bismarck was naturally worried by these developments and also annoyed by French support for Germany's Catholics in their struggle with Falk and himself.

He decided to cut the French down to size. The export of horses to France was forbidden. In April 1875 an article entitled, 'Is War in Sight?' appeared in the government press. France did not, however, drop its plans for an increased army. The new British Prime Minister, Disraeli, who likened Bismarck to Napoleon Bonaparte, decided to interfere, with the unusual support of Russia. The two powers warned Germany that they could not allow France to be beaten a second time. Prince Gortschakov delivered an infuriating sermon to Bismarck in Berlin and then announced 'Peace is assured'. It was thus made to appear that Bismarck, who had had absolutely no intention of attacking France, was being made to back down. The question is then posed, why did Bismarck create this 'war scare' at all? One historian has suggested that it was due to Bismarck's toothache and neuralgia, which made him so short-tempered he wanted to make France share his suffering. The important results were that France and Russia had drawn together a little (an omen for the future), and the League of Three Emperors was shown to be meaningless.

The Congress of Berlin, 1878

The League survived another three years. It could not survive the clash of Russian and Austrian plans in the Balkans. Most of the Balkan peninsula had at one time been part of the Turkish Ottoman Empire. Since 1699, when Hungary gained its independence, the Turks had been steadily losing control over this part of Europe. The peoples of the Balkans were mainly Slavs. Amongst them had grown up a powerful movement, Pan-Slavism, aimed at freeing all Slavs from foreign rule. Since Austria-Hungary also ruled over millions of Slavs it was in her interest to support Turkey against them. Russia on the other hand was a traditional enemy of Turkey. Moreover at this time Russia was developing her industrial power and building many railways, largely with the help of foreign loans. The interest on these loans was repaid by wheat exports but the grain ships had only one ice-free route between Russia and the rest of Europe. This was through the Straits which separate Turkey-in-Europe from Turkey-in-Asia. Russia, therefore, longed to see the Turkish Empire disintegrate and her own forces stationed along the vitally important Straits. Russia's plans were

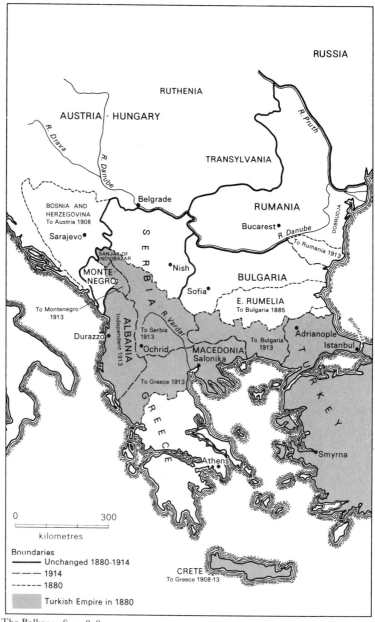

The Balkans after 1878

opposed not only by Austria but also by Britain which feared that Russia might threaten her sea route to India via Suez.

In 1875 some of the Turkish Slav subjects rose in rebellion. The following year the Tsar, Alexander II, decided it was his duty to help the Slavs, who belonged to the same Orthodox Church as did he and most Russians. This new policy was therefore not only anti-Turkish but also anti-Austrian. Both Austria and Russia appealed to Germany for support. Bismarck had absolutely no interest in the Balkans provided there was no threat to peace. He said that it was 'not worth the healthy bones of a Pomeranian musketeer'. Even more worrying to Bismarck were the possible results of a choice between Austria and Russia. The one whom he refused would almost certainly find a ready partner in France. Fortunately Russia and Austria were able to make an agreement. Russia had determined to attack Turkey and Austria agreed not to interfere when Russia promised not to create a new large Slav state from her conquests. Austria was for her part to occupy the provinces of Bosnia-Herzegovina.

Russia's armies quickly overran the Turks and forced Turkey to agree to the creation of a large state – Bulgaria. This infuriated Austria and Britain as well, which saw Bulgaria as a Russian puppet. With British naval forces in the Straits the possibility of war loomed large. This was the possibility which Bismarck feared most. It would be almost impossible for Germany not to join a Balkan War. If Bismarck chose Austria, he would then find himself facing a Franco-Russian alliance. Fortunately for Bismarck, early in 1878 the Austrian foreign minister, Count Andrassy, proposed a European Congress to settle the Balkans problem. Gortschakov agreed; Bismarck offered to act as 'honest broker' and Berlin was chosen for the Congress. It lasted from 13 June to 13 July 1878.

Bismarck thoroughly enjoyed playing host to the leading statesmen of Europe and did his best to dominate the proceedings. 'He bustled through the formal sessions, commenting audibly if the Turkish delegate or even Lord Salisbury dared to raise a new point and scribbling during Gortschakov's opening speech: "Pompos, pompo, pomp, po."'[1] Mealtimes were more important to Bismarck. This was the period when he was

[1] Taylor, *Bismarck*, p. 138.

The Congress of Berlin

still vastly over-eating and one of his most frequent dinner guests was the British Prime Minister, Disraeli. The two men became great friends, each recognizing the other's greatness. The Russians were far less happy. Shuvalov, the Ambassador to London who was the Tsar's chief spokesman, was no match for Disraeli backed by Bismarck. The latter preferred to work behind the scenes and did not begin to play an important role until negotiations deadlocked. The result of the diplomatic haggling was that Russia's plan to create the large state of Bulgaria was dropped. A small principality of Bulgaria and the province of Eastern Roumelia were created instead to take its place.

The Congress of Berlin saved Russia (and Germany) from a disastrous war, but nobody thanked Bismarck for it. The Russians who had defeated Turkey felt that Bismarck had cheated them of their prize. German liberals criticized him for being too kind to Russia; others for weakening the position of Austria. The British also felt that Bismarck had rather favoured Russia. Between 1870 and 1914 relations between Britain and Germany were never better than at the time of this Congress. The League of Three Emperors was at an end. 'I love my uncle, Emperor William,' said the Tsar, 'but Bismarck is a frightful scoundrel.'

But William had been close to death during the Congress following Nobiling's assassination attempt and it was clear to all that
Bismarck was the real ruler of Germany.

Alliances – Dual and Triple

The attacks made on Bismarck by the Russians seemed to bring
out the worst in him. Relations between Germany and Russia
quickly worsened. Imports of Russian cattle were banned following an outbreak of disease in Russia. Wheat imports from
Russia were severely reduced when Bismarck introduced heavy
tariffs on food imports in 1879.

Fresh arrangements were made between Austria and Prussia
for the future of Schleswig. Since Russia's and Denmark's royal
families were blood relatives and the former was not consulted
the Tsar felt he had been slighted. The Russians naturally believed that Austria and Germany had done a deal over Schleswig and the Balkans. To show their fierce resentment the Russians moved up large numbers of troops to the German frontier.
Probably for the first time in his life Bismarck realized the deep-
seated hostility which had existed between Russians and Germans for 500 years. This now convinced him that the only way
to ensure peace for Germany was by a formal alliance with
another great power. With Italy too weak, France and Russia
potentially hostile and Britain unwilling to commit herself, only
Austria-Hungary was a possibility. The Austrians were overjoyed at winning Germany's support against Russia. For his
part Bismarck saw this Dual Alliance as means of warning
Russia and restraining Austria from joining Britain against
Russia. The formal Alliance was signed in October 1879. Both
agreed to help each other if attacked by Russia and to remain
neutral if the other was engaged in a war, say against France,
unless Russia intervened.

In one aspect Bismarck's plan was successful. Russia quickly
lost interest in the Balkans and again turned her attentions to
Central Asia and the Far East. Bismarck's old enemy, Gort-
schakov, retired in 1880 and relations between Berlin and St
Petersburg improved. Austria's plans for an alliance with Bri-
tain came to nothing so Bismarck was able to begin reviving his
League (now called an Alliance) of Three Emperors. The
Alliance was signed in June 1881. Each agreed to remain neut-

ral if one of the others was involved in a war against say Britain
or France. They agreed to keep the Straits closed to foreign
warships and divide the Balkans into 'spheres of influence'.
Austria would be the major power in the West, Russia in the
East. The Alliance particularly pleased the Russians since it
prevented a British naval attack on Russia through the Straits.
Austria was the most unwilling member of the Alliance. However, in 1881 she came to a friendly agreement with Serbia, the
leader of the Pan-Slavs. The following year after a quarrel with
France, Italy joined Austria and Germany in the Triple
Alliance. This threatened France and protected Austria's south-
western frontier from attack by Italy. In 1883 Germany,
Austria and Romania signed a treaty of alliance which was
basically anti-Russian.

During the period 1882–85 Bismarck's policy of 'peace
through alliances' was at its height. Germany was allied with
the three major powers of Central and Eastern Europe and on
good terms with Britain. Moreover, Britain and France were
squabbling over the future of Egypt. Britain had recently sent
an expeditionary force there. A closer examination of Germany's position reveals a less happy position. Bismarck had
again patched up temporarily the quarrel between Austria and
Russia, but the main causes of their quarrel, namely control of
the Straits and Pan-Slavism, remained untouched. Germany
had formal military alliances with Austria and Italy but both
were much weaker than the other three major European powers
(France, Britain and Russia). Neither had a stable government
and both had interests – Austria in the Balkans and Italy in
Africa   which could quickly cause an international flare-up.
Finally of course France might be worried about Egypt and
the war with China in 1884 but Alsace and Lorraine were what
she really cared about. Only Britain was on perfectly good
terms with Germany. Yet in 1883 Bismarck took the surprising
step of seeking to build an overseas colonial Empire in areas
close to British territories.

Germany's Colonial Empire

Bismarck had said publicly on several occasions that he thought
colonies were expensive luxuries. In the early 1870s one French
minister suggested that Bismarck might accept Cochin China

German post in East Africa

(South Vietnam) in exchange for Alsace-Lorraine.[1] Bismarck called it a 'fat morsel' but said Germany was not rich enough for colonies. By the 1880s European nations were seizing colonies in many parts of Africa and Asia. Germany was affected by this desire to build overseas empires. In 1882 the Lord Mayor of Frankfurt founded the Colonial Union to encourage German colonies, and received support from industrialists and merchants who were already trading in remote parts of the world. Missionaries were also active in parts of Africa and adventurers, often with greedy plans, were keen to have Berlin support their schemes.

The first territory to interest the Colonial Union was in South-west Africa, around Walfisch Bay. Bismarck was persuaded to contact London to find whether Britain wanted this territory bordering on her Cape Colony. Letters between Berlin, London and Cape Town often took months to be delivered. In May 1883 a merchant from Bremen, named Adolf Luderitz, hoisted the German flag at Angra Pequena and claimed a strip of the coast for Germany. Eleven months later, with still no firm reply from London, Bismarck lost patience and declared the whole area between Cape Colony and Portuguese Angola to be a German protectorate. A few months later in July 1884

[1] Vietnam was ruled by France from 1862 until 1954.

the territories of Togo and the Cameroons in West Africa became German colonies. The following February Berlin recognized the claim of Karl Peters to 150,000 square kilometres of East Africa (now Tanzania). Thus in a period of less than ten months Germany had gained a large but scattered empire in Africa. At the same time a German expedition claimed the north-eastern part of New Guinea which the Australians had hoped would become British. This territory was renamed *Kaiser-Wilhelms-Land* and one part the *Bismarck-Archipelago*. Apart from Samoa, a few Pacific islands (1889) and the Chinese base of Kiouchou (1898) this was the total of Germany's colonial gains outside Europe.

Germany's African Colonies 1914

Bismarck still had a poor opinion of colonies. During his term of office he refused to turn them into naval or military bases. He made the merchants pay the costs of governing them. Once in 1888, when talking to an explorer, he pointed to a map of Europe and said: 'Here is Russia and here is France and we are in the middle; that is my map of Africa.' Why then did Bismarck take these expensive strips of territory across the world, which Germany could not defend?

It seems to have been very much in Bismarck's favour, both at home and abroad, to be seen to be anti-British at this time. Firstly with an election approaching in 1884 he needed a lever to use against the Socialists and National Liberals. Both opposed the idea of colonies. At the time of the election Britain and Germany might be quarrelling over overseas territories. The Socialists and National Liberals would seem to be supporting Britain if they were not in favour of German annexations. Secondly Kaiser William was eighty-seven years old in 1884 and could not hope to live much longer. The heir to the throne, Crown Prince Frederick, was liberal and pro-British. If Britain and Germany were quarrelling, then it would be extremely difficult for Frederick to develop his friendship for Britain. Bismarck could of course have chosen to develop close ties with Britain but decided that Germany would gain more from a quarrel. Britain's power in the 1880s was not impressive. Her *wartime* military strength was less than 400,000 soldiers compared with the one-and-a-quarter million each of Germany and Russia and the three-quarter million each of France and Austria. In any case Britain's forces were dangerously over-stretched in Egypt, the Sudan, Afghanistan and Burma. The British Navy was still the world's largest but had many out-dated and run-down ships. Bismarck realized quite wisely that if he sided with Britain, the latter's rivals, Russia and France, would be drawn together. Britain would have been quite un-able to help Germany in a two-front land war against the massed French and Russian armies. Bismarck cleverly took advantage of Britain's problems to bully her, thus hoping to win over Britain's other colonial rival France. Co-operation between Germany and France reached its height in 1884–5 when all the great powers, including the USA, met at Berlin to settle the future of Central Africa. Also in 1885 France supported the Triple Alliance in warning Turkey not to allow a British fleet into the Black Sea at a time when an Anglo-Russian war seemed likely.

The Last Five Years

Bismarck's attempt to unite Europe against Britain collapsed quickly in 1885. In France the government of Jules Ferry, which had worked closely with Germany, was defeated in the National Assembly. This came as a result of military defeats in Vietnam. Colonization became unpopular in France. A movement grew up which aimed to recover Alsace-Lorraine. It was called the League of Patriots and its hero a handsome young General, Georges Boulanger. From January 1886 until May 1887 Boulanger was French minister of war.

Within a month or two of Boulanger's appointment he found himself the target of fierce attacks by Bismarck and the German Press which supported the government. Many Germans were led to believe that Boulanger was a second Napoleon Bonaparte ready to lead invading armies over the Rhine. General Waldersee, the Deputy Chief of the German General Staff, privately called Bismarck's talk of war 'a comedy'. Bismarck, however, was preparing to lay a bill before the Reichstag authorizing a 10 per cent increase (40,000 men) in the size of the peacetime army. A 'war scare' was one way of encouraging the Reichstag to accept a larger army. Bismarck secretly realized that France was menaced by the Triple Alliance of Germany, Austria and Italy and still quarrelling fiercely with Britain over Egypt and other territories, and therefore had absolutely no intention of attacking Germany. The dismissal of Boulanger in 1887 showed that France had no wish for war. Bismarck was not in fact worried about France which he was using as a scapegoat, but about Russia, which he dared not publicly attack. For it was yet another Austro-Russian clash in the Balkans which had become the real threat to peace in Europe.

In September 1885 Prince Alexander of Battenberg, the ruler of Bulgaria, had taken over the province of Eastern Roumelia. Although this union had been forbidden by the Congress of Berlin in 1878, the Russians were infuriated because the prince was strongly anti-Russian. Thinking that the enlarged Bulgaria might have plans to seize her territory, Serbia attacked her but was heavily defeated.

Serbia was then saved from invasion by Austria. At this point Russia intervened again and an Austro-Russian clash loomed. Bismarck was greatly angered to see his intricate alliance system break down. He put the blame solely on Alexander and persecuted him until his death. Meanwhile Bismarck warned Austria not to expect any help from Germany if she fought Russia. The situation was improving until Prince Alexander was kidnapped by Russian officers and eventually forced to abdicate. It was generally believed that Russia would then invade Bulgaria and Austria would fight. Some leading German generals, such as Waldersee, favoured an immediate attack on Russia before the

Count Waldersee

latter's plans to enlarge her army were complete. Bismarck was shocked by this suggestion and worked hard to restore international calm. Some Germans accused him of 'crawling to the Russians'. Bismarck's efforts to restore peace consisted, as usual, of fresh treaties and alliances. During the first half of 1887 no less than three treaties were drawn up, two of which Germany signed and the third she supported.

In February 1887 the Triple Alliance of Germany, Austria and Italy was renewed. Italy made Germany promise to support her if she fought a colonial war with France and to make France hand over certain territories after such a war. The main agreement amongst the three powers was to resist any frontier changes in the Balkans. Fortunately for Bismarck the possibility of a Franco-Italian war was reduced by a new treaty, the Mediterranean *Entente*, signed in March. The purpose of the treaty, masterminded by Britain and signed also by Austria and Italy, was to prevent both France and Russia increasing their power in the Eastern Mediterranean or the Balkans. Bismarck was well pleased. Once more he had isolated France, frozen the situation in the Balkans and had even associated Britain rather loosely with the Triple Alliance. Nevertheless he was still worried about Russia's strength.

He continued to work for better relations with St Petersburg. Since January 1887 he had been holding talks with Paul Shuvalov, the Russian Ambassador to Berlin, and his brother Peter. Their talks led to a Reinsurance Treaty, valid for three years from June 1887. The two powers agreed not to fight unless Russia attacked Austria or Germany attacked France. However, in a highly secret clause Bismarck promised to support the Tsar if he felt it necessary to seize the Straits by force! Thus in the Triple Alliance Bismarck promised to prevent changes in the Balkans but in the Reinsurance Treaty to allow Russia to make changes. Far from putting him in an impossible position Bismarck's alliances were really designed to cancel themselves out. If everything went according to his wishes, no single treaty could come into operation without bringing others into play which would prevent the first from working. 'Thus wars would be, so to speak, throttled at birth or would, at worst, remain localized.'[1]

[1] Richter, *Bismarck*, p. 296.

The possibility of war was reduced in 1888 following the new treaties. But Germany and Russia, despite the Reinsurance Treaty, found themselves increasingly disagreeing. The Tsar was surrounded by advisers who wanted stronger support for the Pan-Slavs and a military alliance with France. Bismarck was warned by the Austrian Emperor, Francis-Joseph, that kindness and friendship was wasted on the Russians. The decisive break came with an order from the Tsar forbidding foreigners to buy land in western Russia. Bismarck replied by preventing Russia borrowing German money for railway building and industrial projects. French banks, encouraged by their government, were only too happy to lend to Russia. In October 1888 the Russians received their first French loan. These totalled £500 million by 1917 and were never repaid. The following January (1889) Russia began buying French arms.

By 1889 Bismarck must have realized that once he retired a Franco-Russian alliance would follow. For it was only his personality and reputation which kept alive the Berlin–St Petersburg link.

His thoughts turned naturally to Britain, the great rival of France and Russia in Africa and Asia respectively. Discussions about an Anglo-German alliance were held in London. The difficulty was, how could Germany help Britain in a war with Russia over India or how could the Royal Navy save Germany in a two-front land war? Britain was still suspicious of Bismarck for the colonial troubles of 1884–5 and for his alliances. Whatever the real reason, probably German unwillingness to fight Russia, the talks failed; perhaps the greatest tragedy of the nineteenth century, for if an alliance based on genuine friendship and understanding could have been arranged between the world's greatest land and sea powers a major war would not have been possible.

During 1889 and early 1890 Bismarck was busy with other problems: strikes, the anti-socialist law and his pensions bill. The Reinsurance Treaty was due for renewal in June 1890. However, many weeks earlier Bismarck had, after an angry dispute, offered his resignation and had it accepted by the young Emperor, William II.

6 New Masters

Frederick III

The winter of 1887–8 was particularly cold and bitter throughout Europe. The health of the Emperor had been poor for more than two years. He could walk only with the aid of a stick and even so he sometimes fell over and could not get up without help. Towards the end of the long, bitter winter William I developed a cold and on Tuesday 5 March 1888 he collapsed. It was soon obvious he had no strength left. The Emperor's grandson, Prince William, hurried home from Italy to the sickbed. On Thursday the Emperor was visited by the Grand Duke and Duchess of Baden and at noon he had his last conversation with Bismarck. During the afternoon William grew weaker and became delirious. By 5 p.m. most of the royal family and leading members of the government were at the Emperor's bedside. In broken sentences the dying man talked of his military campaigns, his regiments and individual officers and soldiers. After the issue of the last bulletin at 9 p.m. few watchers outside the Palace remained in the bitter cold. At 3 a.m. an urgent message brought Prince William, Bismarck and von Moltke back to the Palace at high speed. Still the old Emperor struggled for life and after three hours Bismarck and von Moltke returned home. Finally at 8.30 a.m. on 8 March 1888 it was all over. The flag over the Palace was lowered to half-mast and telegrams were sent to all the capitals of the world.

The Reichstag met at noon. 'Every deputy was in his seat and the gallery full of spectators. But a solemn silence reigned throughout the spacious hall, each man only communing with his own sad thoughts or casting a sidelong glance at his neighbour to divine his sombre meditations.'[1] Bismarck entered wearing his Cuirassier's uniform and Prussia's highest award *Ordre pour le Merite*. He was accompanied by his son Herbert. 'It is my mournful duty', he said, 'to convey to you the official announcement of what you are already in point of fact aware – namely that His Majesty the Emperor William I was

[1] *The Times*, 10 March 1888.

gathered to his fathers this morning at half-past eight o'clock. In consequence of this event the Prussian crown together with the Imperial Dignity has now passed to His Majesty Frederick III, King of Prussia.' Bismarck spoke for a few more minutes then the President of the Reichstag rose to close the sitting.

In Berlin everything halted. The Town Council assembled and immediately dispersed. The Stock Exchange remained closed as did theatres and other places of entertainment. The university term, with only a few days left, was declared at an end. All school classes were dismissed. All over Europe and even in New York flags hung at half mast. In London *The Times* devoted three pages of close print, edged in black, to the obituary and last hours of the German Emperor. In Athens the Hellenic Royal Court declared a six-week period of mourning.

The body of William lay in state guarded by eight colonels until the state funeral a week after his death. The service was held in the Dom, Berlin's Cathedral. The front of the building was draped in enormous black tapestries bearing the royal coat-of-arms and other decorations. Between the entrance pillars stood enormous imitation candles, four metres high and fired by gas. The streets were lined with troops and police to hold

The funeral of William I .

back the vast crowds which, despite the icy winds, had gathered along the route of the funeral procession and the neighbouring streets. By contrast with the bustling and noisy streets the Cathedral was a scene of reverence and quiet. Behind the coffin draped in crimson and gold velvet stood row upon row of the members of Europe's royal houses, generals, statesmen and ambassadors. Among the most distinguished were the Prince of Wales (the future Edward VII) and the Tsarevitch (the future Nicholas II, who would be executed by the Bolsheviks in 1918). Bismarck was not to be seen amongst the mourners. Probably the strain of the previous two weeks, and the personal grief at losing the man whom he had served for twenty-six years, was too great.

The service began promptly at noon, interrupted in the later stages by several volleys of distant rifle-fire, the army's last salute. Despite the bitter cold the crowds were well-disciplined until the arrival of privileged groups of workers, students and army veterans. These were allocated places five or six deep in front of the earlier arrivals, poor citizens who had waited patiently since dawn. Fighting broke out until a charge of mounted police restored order.

The funeral procession took more than an hour to pass. It was headed by the cavalry regiments – Hussars, Dragoons and Uhlans – followed by the infantry. Pride of place here was given to Russian and Austrian grenadiers, with German regiments leading the hearse. Much of the colour and splendour of the occasion was lost by the need to wear greatcoats and hats in the freezing temperatures. The coffin was taken to the royal mausoleum at Charlottenburg Castle. Eventually a 101-gun salute signalled the end of the funeral.

Bismarck's absence was, surprisingly, not the most noticeable. The new Emperor, Frederick III, had seen only the last minutes of the funeral from an upstairs window at Charlottenburg. The reason for his absence was understood and appreciated even more sympathetically than Bismarck's; for Frederick III was a dying man. Indeed for some time there had been doubt whether he would survive his father to ascend the throne.

Born at Potsdam in 1831, Frederick was the only son of William I and the Empress Augusta. He had entered the Army at the age of seven and became a 2nd lieutenant three years

The Royal Palace at Potsdam

later. His promotion was rapid. To celebrate the fall of Sedan in 1870 William created his son Field-Marshal, the first Prussian prince to achieve this distinction. In between his campaigns and sitting on committees Frederick found time to woo and marry Princess Victoria, the eldest daughter of Queen Victoria. They had two sons and four daughters, two other sons dying in infancy. Frederick was a man of liberal ideas, which had made him the enemy of Bismarck. Nevertheless, as a Prussian officer and Crown Prince the dignity of the monarchy and the state were more important to him.

In January 1887 Frederick developed an inflammation of the throat and a persistent cough. He could talk only in a hoarse whisper. Normal treatments including taking the waters at Ems did nothing to relieve these symptoms. His doctors were convinced that he was suffering from cancer of the throat and proposed an operation to remove the complete larynx. This suggestion was so serious that it was decided to call in the world's foremost throat specialist from London, Sir Morell Mackenzie. On 22 May Sir Morell successfully removed a piece of tissue

83

from the Prince's throat for examination under a microscope. It was announced that the examination had not proved cancer. It now seems certain that this was a lie. Sir Morell lied to save the Prince from the operation which would almost certainly have killed him from septicaemia.

In June 1887 Frederick was warmly received in London for Queen Victoria's golden jubilee. Afterwards he stayed at Osborn House on the Isle of Wight and Balmoral in Scotland. In the autumn he moved with his family to the warmer climate of San Remo, in Italy. Here his condition worsened. A swelling, caused by a thickening of the mucous membrane of the larynx, appeared on his throat. By February 1888 the swelling was threatening to cut off the air supply through the windpipe and an operation became urgent. This was carried out without an anaesthetic but the Prince bore it bravely as he had done all along. A small curved silver tube was inserted into his throat to provide an extra air supply. By this time, of course, he had completely lost his speech and had to communicate by written notes.

When the Emperor William I died in March 1888 Frederick immediately returned to Berlin by special train. As Emperor he was almost completely under Bismarck's influence as his father had been. He had long since accepted an early death and knew that his plans and hopes would never be realized. Bismarck remarked that despite the change of crowns business was going 'as smoothly as a game of roulette'. Soon after becoming Emperor Frederick was again confined to bed with bronchitis. One of his visitors was his mother-in-law, Queen Victoria.

The power-struggle between the royal family and the Chancellor was carried on by the new Empress, Victoria. Bismarck regarded her liberal views as a menace to the future of the Prussian monarchy, and treated her accordingly. Victoria had become fond of Prince Alexander of Battenberg, the handsome former head of state of Bulgaria. She determined to arrange a marriage between Alexander and her daughter, also called Victoria. Also she demanded that Alexander be made a general, given command of the famous regiment, the *Gardekorps*, and be awarded a very high decoration. Bismarck, who still blamed Alexander for the Bulgarian crisis which had nearly shattered the peace in 1885, was enraged. He knew that the Tsar, who also loathed Alexander, would be angry with Germany. Accordingly Bismarck put great pressure upon both the dying Emperor and Prince Alexander's elder relations to ban the marriage. He succeeded.

Frederick had decided to spend his last days in the Palace at Potsdam where he was born. Early in June 1888 he made his last journey across the River Havel and here at Potsdam made his one independent gesture as Emperor. He had learnt that the Prussian Minister of the Interior, von Puttkamer, had been guilty of fraud at a recent election. Frederick ordered him to be

The funeral of Frederick III

dismissed and, against the wishes of Bismarck, this was done. Frederick retired to his bed on 13 June. He could no longer swallow properly and he was losing weight. As the post-mortem later revealed gangrene had set in and quickly reached his lungs. On the 15th, a beautiful summer's day, at shortly after 11 a.m., Frederick III, Emperor for ninety-nine days, died.

Berlin became again a city in mourning. The trappings of black crêpe reappeared and the flags flew at half-mast. In the capitals of Europe crown princes, grand dukes, generals and premiers boarded their special trains to Berlin. The mourners, led by the new Emperor William II and the Prince of Wales, each resplendent in the uniform of a Prussian General, assembled in the Hall of Shells at Potsdam. Again Bismarck was absent from a royal funeral but few were ready to believe that

85

ill-health or personal grief were the reason this time. To Bismarck the reign of Frederick III and his English wife was merely an irritating episode now thankfully over.

William II

As soon as possible Bismarck left Berlin for his estate at Friedrichsruh where he remained throughout the summer, keeping in touch with the government by telegraph. The new Emperor was busy on a series of state visits to Vienna, Rome and St Petersburg, where he enjoyed immensely being the centre of attraction. Bismarck left the young man alone, thinking that he in turn would be left in peace to govern the German Empire until his death. William II had other ideas. A few weeks after becoming Emperor he said, 'I shall let the old man snuffle on for six months, then I shall rule myself'. Bismarck made no attempt to gain the friendship of the young Emperor. He either ignored him or poured scorn on his suggestions. Most of the time the two were physically far apart. Bismarck's absence from Berlin after Frederick's funeral lasted eight months. He returned in January 1889 and left again in May after speaking about his pensions bill in the Reichstag. Apart from the occasional day he did not come back to Berlin until January 1890.

By the time Bismarck returned, the differences of opinion between himself and the young Kaiser had become too wide to be papered over. Mainly they argued about social welfare measures. Bismarck cared nothing for popularity. William II wanted desperately to be loved and honoured by all classes of German society. This had been clearly shown during the great coal strike of May 1889. Bismarck naturally sided with the employers. William, on learning of the very poor living conditions of the miners, summoned the coal-owners and ordered them to raise the miners' wages. William planned social reforms such as banning child labour, reducing working hours and ending Sunday working. These plans were put forward to a meeting of the Crown Council in January 1890. Bismarck, whose ideas on economics had been created forty years previously, opposed laws against what he called the 'workers' right to make an income'. He suggested that the Kaiser's proposals be examined by a committee of ministers. To this William reluctantly agreed.

William II in naval uniform

The next issue for discussion was even more difficult. This was Bismarck's proposal to make the anti-Socialist law permanent. Since 1887 Bismarck had had many supporters in the Reichstag but now his supporters were split. The National Liberals refused to vote for the anti-Socialist law if it gave powers to the police to drive Socialists from their homes. The Conservatives refused to vote for it unless this clause was kept in. Bismarck suggested that the law should lapse, hoping that the Socialists would then rise in rebellion and the army could be called in to crush the movement once and for all. William naturally had no wish to have the first years of his reign remembered for bloodshed. Although the ministers reluctantly supported Bismarck by agreeing that Socialists could lose their homes, the latter must have realized that he would not be able to continue in office much longer on these terms.

The results of the election of 20 February 1890 showed clearly that Bismarck was losing support. His supporters in the Reichstag were greatly reduced. These were the Conservatives who lost 17 seats, the Reichspartei, 19, and the National Liberals, 57. The Centre Party gained 8 and the Progressives 44, while the Social Democrats more than tripled their numbers to gain 35 seats. Bismarck did not even consider resignation. Instead he produced the most outlandish plot of his career. Two major bills, he decided, would be laid before the Reichstag. One would call for an increase in the army of 125,000 men; the other for a permanent and brutal anti-Socialist law. Both would probably be rejected by the Reichstag. Then an Assembly of German Princes would meet to alter the constitution. The Reichstag would lose most of its powers and voting rights would be greatly reduced. Bismarck was, in his bid to regain his position, virtually suggesting the wrecking of the Empire which he had struggled so hard to build and preserve. Fortunately William II rejected this plan out of hand and refused to agree to further anti-Socialist legislation.

The relationship between the aged Chancellor and the thirty-one-year old Emperor was by this time at a very low point. Two further incidents reduced it to breaking-point. First, Bismarck rediscovered an order of 1852 issued by Frederick William IV forbidding ministers to approach the king without first consulting the Minister-President. Obviously Bismarck saw this as an excellent means of preventing the Kaiser and other ministers meeting to overthrow him. Soon after this the leader of the Centre Party, Ludgwig Windthorst, approached Bismarck with the offer of support. This threatened William's plan to get rid of Bismarck. Naturally the news of the meeting quickly reached the Kaiser. Two days later William went to the Chancellery early in the morning and demanded to see Bismarck. A furious argument developed between the two men, ranging over all their differences of the previous weeks. Suddenly Bismarck brought up the subject of William's proposed visit to Russia and said he could not go because of unpleasant reports he had received from the German Ambassador. William demanded to see these reports and went white with shock when he read them. In one letter the Tsar had called him 'an ill-bred youngster of bad faith'. However, he composed himself and before leaving told Bismarck he wanted the 1852 cabinet order to be withdrawn.

During the next forty-eight hours Bismarck received two visits from General Hahnke, chief of the military cabinet. On the first he demanded the abolition of the 1852 order; on the second not only the abolition but also Bismarck's resignation. A few hours later another messenger arrived and asked Bismarck for his resignation. Bismarck replied that he must have time to compose his letter, wondering how the squabble over a forty-year old order could possibly be made to explain the differences between the young Emperor and Europe's greatest statesman.

Then luck returned to Bismarck. The German Consul in Kiev had reported great Russian military manœuvres. Bismarck usually ignored such reports, but William made an enormous fuss demanding that Austria be informed at once. Bismarck at once saw his way of escape. The Emperor could be accused of meddling in foreign affairs. Bismarck used this as his reason for resigning, speaking of the Emperor's 'new policy towards Russia'. William was attending a musical recital at the castle when Bismarck's resignation arrived. He wrote a brief reply in pencil and went back to his music. When told of the news the aged Count von Moltke commented aptly: 'Very regrettable: the young gentleman will yet present us with many riddles'.

On 24 March Bismarck found General Caprivi, his successor, inspecting the Chancellery. It was time to go. He took a cold and formal farewell of the Emperor, held a small dinner-party of close friends and began to pack his possessions which included 13,000 bottles of wine. On the 27th he went to Charlottenburg and laid three roses on the tomb of William I. On 29 March 1890 he drove through the crowded but silent streets of Berlin to the Lehrter station. As the train pulled out to the accompaniment of a military band Bismarck stood at the open window of his carriage and passed from history into retirement.

Bismarck in Retirement

Two days after arriving at Friedrichsruh Bismarck celebrated his seventy-fifth birthday. He received greetings and presents from all parts of Europe. William II's present was an enormous

Bismarck in retirement

portrait of himself! Bismarck was then free to settle down to the life of a country gentleman. He became very interested in the migration of birds and spent many hours walking or riding round his estates, receiving his usual greetings from the country-people: 'Herr Furst' (Mr Prince).

Bismarck's retirement greatly affected the life of his son Herbert. At the early age of forty Herbert had to resign his post as Foreign Secretary and retire to manage the family estates at Schönhausen. The family plan had been for Herbert to take over as Imperial Chancellor after his father's death. Instead Herbert had to be content with a seat in the Reichstag, where he adopted a pro-Russian and anti-British attitude. He married in 1892, fathered three children and died at an early age in 1904.

Like many other great men since his time, Bismarck was persuaded to write his memoirs. The Stuttgart publishers, Cotta, requested six volumes with a fee of £5,000 per volume. Bismarck began work in July 1890 dictating to Lothar Bucher, a former Foreign Office executive. The result, entitled *Reflections and Reminiscences*, was disappointing. Bismarck selected events from his career almost at random. He naturally wanted to prove himself right even though this led to his repeating himself and including many mistakes. There was little about his personal or family life to interest the general reader. After finishing the first two volumes Bucher died and Bismarck lost interest. The six volumes were eventually published between 1898 and 1907; an English translation of the first two also appeared in 1898.

Bismarck found retirement dull and decided to return to politics as a Reichstag deputy. He managed to get himself elected as a National Liberal but never actually entered the Reichstag. Instead he turned to journalism and received a free hand to write articles for a Hamburg paper. During 1892 over a hundred pieces of his work appeared, many attacking General Caprivi, the Chancellor, and the Kaiser. William replied by ceasing to send birthday and Christmas presents to Bismarck. He also tried to have Bismarck officially ignored when he went to Vienna for Herbert's wedding in 1892. In fact Bismarck's welcome in the Austrian capital was enormous. His popularity in Germany amongst ordinary people, particularly in the countryside, was quite unchanged by his fall from power. Streets were named after him and statues of him erected in almost every German town. Pilgrimages and railway excursions were made to Friedrichsruh. 'Souvenirs of Bismarck' were on sale everywhere in the village. At public gatherings he was the centre of attraction and was addressed by such titles as 'Hail, Otto the Great'.

Nevertheless his political power had ended. In 1894 William II invited him to dine at the Palace in Berlin and for support Bismarck took along his sons, Herbert and Bill. The conversation never touched politics and Bismarck returned home a little disappointed. No German politician visited Friedrichsruh until Tirpitz, the architect of Germany's battle-fleet, arrived to tell of his plans. Even Bismarck's eightieth birthday celebrations in 1895 were spoilt by the refusal of the Reichstag to send a message of congratulation.

It is most unlikely that Bismarck could ever have been a politician again, for his health was beginning to fail. He was unable to ride after 1892 and soon walking left him very tired. He was deeply saddened by the death of his wife Johanna in 1894. Apart from recurrent pains in his facial nerves his greatest sufferings were in his legs, the result of his injury in Russia nearly forty years previously. He began to develop severe pains in the toes and these moved through the feet to the ankle. Professor Schweniger, who still attended Bismarck, diagnosed gangrene but managed to check its spread. By 1897 Bismarck could walk only a dozen paces with assistance and spent most of the day in a wheelchair. In July 1898 he again contracted inflammation of the lungs. He developed an unquenchable thirst and was kept alive for a short time by camphor injections. On 31 July at 11 a.m. he died.

Kaiser William was cruising off Norway in the Royal Yacht when the news arrived. He hurried back to Germany and laid a wreath on the sealed coffin in Friedrichsruh. A memorial service was held in Berlin on 3 August, an intensely hot day. Only a small crowd gathered outside the Emperor William Memorial Church and there were empty seats within. Bismarck had ordered that a special mausoleum should be built for the bodies of Johanna and himself but this was not completed until the following spring. His coffin, therefore, remained in his room at Friedrichsruh for eight months. He was finally buried, in the presence of William II, on 1 April 1899 on what would have been his eighty-fourth birthday.

William's arrival at Friedrichsruh

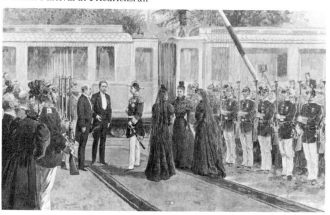

7 Prince William

The Royal Recruit

William II, the Emperor who brought Bismarck's political career to a close in 1890, was born in the royal palace in Berlin on 27 January 1859. His English-born mother, Princess Victoria, then only eighteen years old, almost died giving him birth. Marshal Wrangel, mistaking the moment, drove his fist through the palace window and shouted, 'it's a braw recruit'. An artillery salvo was immediately fired and the Emperor William I, then the Prussian Prince Regent, ran out of his house and hailed a cab in his eagerness to reach the palace. Meanwhile the doctors were still fighting to save Victoria's life and when the new Prince was actually born no one noticed for some time that his left arm had been wrenched out of its socket. By then it was too late. Despite painful electrical treatments the arm hung almost useless. William's jackets were cut with the left arm shorter than the right and a special combination knife and fork was designed to enable him to eat with one hand.

A week after his birth the baby prince was christened Friedrich Wilhelm Viktor Albrecht. Queen Victoria was prevented from seeing her first grandchild by political trouble in England. William was twenty months old before Victoria was able to visit Prussia to see him. 'He is a fine fat child', she wrote, 'with beautiful white soft skin, very fine shoulders and limbs and a very dear face. He has Fritz's (Crown Prince Frederick) eyes and Vicky's (Princess Victoria) very fair curly hair.' Royal christenings became regular events in Prussia during the next few years for Princess Victoria provided William with three brothers and four sisters, though one of each died in infancy.

At the age of two and a half years William made his first of many visits to Britain. His second visit at the age of four was for the royal wedding at Windsor of the future Edward VII and Princess Alexandra of Denmark. For this occasion the little prince wore a Highland costume and was reported to have threatened an English uncle with his dirk. He also threw his sporran into the aisle!

William seems to have enjoyed his visits to Britain for his grandmother, Queen Victoria, spoilt him greatly. In Berlin his father, Crown Prince Frederick, was too busy with official duties to have much time for him, other than taking his children on an occasional picnic. Princess Victoria also tended to neglect him in his early years. Admittedly she had a succession of babies to attend to but Victoria had become very interested in Prussian politics. She wanted to convert Prussia to the British system of government. The arrival of Queen Victoria and three British ministers only six months after the princess's marriage to Frederick strengthened this view of the princess among Prussians. It was not surprising that Princess Victoria and Bismarck became bitter foes.

The Student

Like most young people of high rank William was looked after first by a nurse (who was British) and then by a governess (who was German). The latter, Fraulein von Dobeneck, was, to quote William, 'a great gaunt dame of firm character whose method by no means excluded the use of the palm'. At the age of seven William was put in the care of a tutor, George Hintzpeter, who was responsible for the prince's education until he was twenty. Hintzpeter was a gloomy unsmiling man who believed firmly in the values of hard work and self-denial. Lessons for the young prince began at six or seven in the morning and often went on for twelve hours. The main subjects were the classical languages, Greek and Latin. These, believed Hintzpeter, would ensure that the prince would become a thoughtful, knowledgeable and intelligent man. Of his years of studying classics William wrote 'We tortured ourselves over thousands of pages of grammar'. In addition he studied history, but only as late as the year 1648, mathematics, English and French. He became very fluent in English, having plenty of opportunity for practice, and also picked up some Russian and Italian. Hintzpeter controlled every aspect of the young prince's upbringing. William was taught self-control by having to hand cakes to his friends but refuse them himself.

Hintzpeter hoped to develop the prince's character and courage by teaching him to ride. It was also vital for the future king of a great military nation to be able to ride well on cere-

Prince William aged 10

monial occasions. William was virtually one-armed; also he was naturally nervous and would mount a horse only if it was led by a groom. Eventually Hintzpeter ordered him to mount without stirrups or groom and then told him to move the horse forward. Within seconds William fell off and was promptly reseated. Again and again William fell off and despite his tears and the howls of his younger brother, Henry, he was forced to remount. Riding lessons must have been a most painful business for William, still not ten years old, but eventually he gained his balance and became a good rider. He soon had the opportunity to use his new skill. In 1869 he was commissioned as a second lieutenant in the Pomeranian Regiment and rode in the last review before it left for the French war. In 1871 he took his place in the triumphant parade to celebrate the return of the newly-crowned German Emperor to Berlin.

In addition to riding William also learnt to swim, and he was taught tennis by the daughters of a British ambassador at The Hague. Surprisingly he became a good shot, bagging his first pheasant at the age of thirteen and his first deer four years later. His mother regretted that he could not run fast, blaming his lack of balance. Nevertheless he appears to have overcome his handicap quite well. In fact he may have used up so much energy in this struggle that he had little left for other purposes. He was certainly not an outstanding scholar. Hintzpeter attached to him that famous schoolmaster's label 'lacks concentration'. William found the long arduous routine in the schoolroom difficult to bear. He escaped by daydreaming of the military glory of the new Empire, for it was between his fifth and twelfth birthdays that Prussia won its three victories over Denmark, Austria and France. William read magazines, studied war maps and collected photographs of his grandfather's coronation and other glorious events.

Hintzpeter became convinced that the only way to bring William back to reality was to have him mix with boys from more ordinary families. He spent months trying to persuade Princess Victoria to his point of view. Finally he succeeded, but Prussia's nobility were shocked to learn in 1874 that the two eldest sons of the Crown Prince were to attend Kassel Gymnasium.[1] William himself was not at all pleased at the idea of having to mix with strange boys and risk being beaten by them in examinations. Hintzpeter also decided that, far from travelling in state, he and the two princes would hike over the mountains to Kassel. The three eventually arrived in the town looking like tramps and had some difficulty in proving their identities. However, William and his brother Henry settled down quite well in Kassel enjoying the friendly rivalries of school life. William was not willing to forget his position, nor would he allow his classmates to forget. Hintzpeter stayed in Kassel with William during his three years at the Gymnasium and arranged weekly dinner parties with distinguished guests for the prince's benefit. It is doubtful if William had much energy for these social gatherings for studies at the Gymnasium began two hours before breakfast and continued until 8 p.m. Again William showed that he had no more than average ability, finishing

[1] Equivalent to an English grammar school.

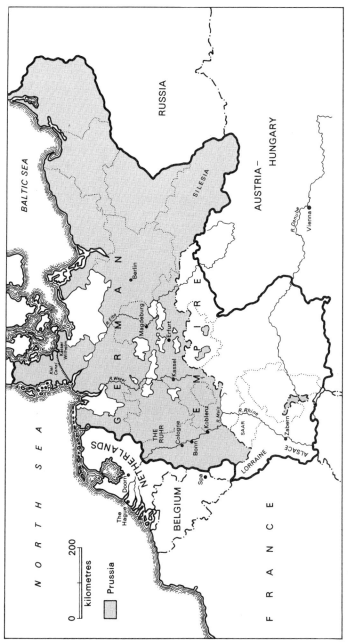

William II's Germany

tenth out of seventeen in his final examinations in 1877.

William had now almost 'come of age' at eighteen years and like all young men in Prussia had to do six months' military service. Meanwhile it was announced that the Emperor intended to give him the Order of the Black Eagle and Queen Victoria intended to make him a Grand Companion of the Order of Bath. William did not think a G.C.B. was sufficient and through his mother made it known to Queen Victoria that he wanted the Order of the Garter. Queen Victoria agreed. It was also discussed whether he should attend Balliol College, Oxford, but instead in 1878 he went to the University of Bonn for four terms. He studied history, economics, politics and law, and again showed little interest in studying. One of his tutors said that William believed he knew everything without having learnt anything. He joined a students' club, the Borussia, but, unlike Bismarck, fought no duels. He was, however, quick to criticize fellow students for drunkenness and immorality.

Whilst studying at Bonn William frequently visited the home of his mother's sister Princess Alice, Grand Duchess of Hesse-Darmstadt. The restless young prince did not make himself very popular with Alice's children, but evidently he fell in love with one of the daughters, Elisabeth, a very attractive girl of fifteen. William spent much of his spare time composing love poems to her. The royal family did not like the idea of William marrying a cousin, although his brother Henry married Elisabeth's sister Irene in 1888. In 1880 the disappointed William suddenly announced he wished to marry Princess Augusta-Victoria of Schleswig-Holstein. His mother favoured the idea, hoping that marriage would make him less rude and boastful and more tolerant. A year later on 25 February 1881 William and Augusta were married in Berlin. Elisabeth eventually married a Russian grand duke.

The Prussian Officer

William and his new bride lived for a year in an old castle until their official home, the Marble Palace in Potsdam, was ready for them. For nearly two years, since leaving Bonn, William had been a full-time soldier serving in the Guards as a lieutenant. A few months after his marriage he was promoted major and transferred to the cavalry. Despite his crippled arm he proved an able officer, leading his men through complicated manœuvres without difficulty. William found that marriage and an honourable career in the army had freed him from the control of his parents. He was also able to enjoy life much more. He was particularly happy in the company of his brother officers on Mess nights. He attended receptions and banquets and beer evenings at the house of General Versen. On Wednesday evenings he attended prayer meetings organized by the 'political General' Count von Waldersee. Association with Waldersee

William and Augusta-Victoria

led him to the Chancellor's household where Bismarck often had long conversations with him. In 1884 Bismarck chose William rather than his father, the Crown Prince, to visit Moscow for the coming-of-age celebrations of the Tsarevitch Nicholas.

This was the beginning of the 'Willy–Nicky' friendship which lasted until 1914. William pleased Tsar Alexander with his talk of a Triple Alliance of Emperors against the threat of anarchy, democracy and socialism. Henceforth, William became steadily more involved in the politics of the German Empire. He wrote a secret letter to the Tsar warning him of British treachery and openly opposed the marriage of one of Queen Victoria's daughters to Prince Henry of Battenberg. The result of these actions was a further serious rift between William and his parents. Bismarck, who greatly disliked Crown Prince Frederick and Victoria, naturally encouraged William's line of action. In 1886 Bismarck sent William to the meeting of the three Emperors at Gastein and also allowed him to read state papers. The latter privilege was bitterly opposed by the Crown Prince, who had never been granted it himself. In a letter to Bismarck, Frederick asked him to reconsider, stating that William was vain, boastful and lacking in judgment. By this time William and his father were scarcely on speaking terms and by a cruel stroke of fate this situation soon became permanent with the development of Crown Prince Frederick's throat cancer early in 1887.

With his grandfather, the aged Emperor William I, growing weaker and his father fatally ill in San Remo, Prince William was, by the end of 1887, virtually 'deputy Emperor'. Some of William's friends suggested that if his grandfather died first, he should succeed directly to the Imperial throne instead of his father. William agreed that 'it is very questionable if a man who cannot speak has any right whatever to become king of Prussia'. Probably he never seriously considered such a plan and his natural love for his father made him worry about his health. When he heard that doctors were being rushed to his father, William realized that Sir Morell Mackenzie's diagnosis had been wrong. William suspected that his mother had deliberately employed an English doctor to hide the truth from his father in case he decided not to become Emperor. William hurried to San Remo to learn the truth. Princess Victoria thought William's visit rude and ill-timed and told him so, but Frederick was happy to see his eldest son again and the two drew closer together than they had been for many years.

William did not seem willing to wait quietly until his father died and then ascend the throne. Both he and Bismarck put the blame for the Crown Prince's condition on Mackenzie and the official press became hostile toward Mackenzie, the Crown Princess and Britain in general. After the death of his grandfather, William made a speech comparing the Empire to an army. The commander was dead, the second-in-command gravely wounded so all must rally round the senior surviving officer, he said. When his father finally died two months later William ordered his troops to surround the palace where the Emperor lay and a desperate search was made for Frederick's diaries and papers. William thought they might contain

William at Army manoeuvres

important secrets. These, however, had been secretly passed to the British ambassador some days before. William then took the funeral arrangements out of his mother's hands, having already added to her distress by ordering a post-mortem on Frederick's body.

In his first public speech as Kaiser, William II addressed himself not to the German people but to the army: 'We belong to each other – I and the army,' he said; 'we were born for each other and will always remain loyal to each other, whether it be the will of God to send us calm or storm.' Altogether William's entry into German political life had been neither graceful nor promising for the future peace and happiness of the Empire. Queen Victoria considered her grandson to be in a 'very unhealthy and unnatural state of mind' and that he might 'at ANY moment become impossible!'

Lord Salisbury, the British prime minister, discussing the situation with a French minister, said, '*There* is a dark cloud.'[1]

[1] Balfour, *The Kaiser and His Times*, p. 123.

8 William and Europe
1890–1900

Germany and Russia

The fall of Bismarck brought about the greatest changes in Germany's foreign policy. William was uncertain about the future position of Germany in Europe and neither his ministers nor the leading members of the Foreign Service had Bismarck's complete understanding of foreign affairs. The first result of Bismarck's fall was the cutting of the 'line to St Petersburg'. Baron Holstein, a leading Foreign Office official, who was determined to take Bismarck's place in foreign affairs, persuaded the Government not to renew the 1887 Reinsurance Treaty with Russia. Holstein said that Germany could not have treaties with both Austria and Russia which contradicted each other. While refusing to sign any agreements with Russia, Germany was coming to terms with Britain over colonial matters. It was agreed, in 1890, that Britain should restore Heligoland to Germany which in turn would recognize British authority in Zanzibar. This treaty was very unpopular in Germany since it was giving away colonies instead of getting new ones. The Russians saw it as a prelude to Britain's joining the Triple Alliance. This fear, coming soon after the fall of Bismarck, a friend of Russia, convinced the Tsar and his advisers that their future safety lay with France.

The idea of a Franco-Russian alliance had been discussed in both countries for many years but the first definite moves did not come until 1888. Following the ending of the Reichsbank loans, the Russians turned to France (p. 79). With the building of the trans-Siberian Railway in the 1890s the Russian need for French capital increased. Russia also began to buy arms from France. William II said to the Russian ambassador Shuvalov: 'You know how I love and respect the Tsar . . . my foreign policy will remain the same as my grandfather's.' But this was not enough to convince the Russians that Germany was not becoming hostile. In August 1891 the French fleet visited the

Russian naval base at Kronstadt in the Baltic. The Tsar himself welcomed the French and stood solemnly to attention as the band played the *Marseillaise*, the music of the French Revolution. Military talks followed in 1892, and in October 1893 the Russian fleet made a return visit, receiving a tremendous welcome at the French port of Toulon. By early 1894 a full-scale Franco-Russian military alliance had been signed. Bismarck's policy of isolating France was in ruins and Germany faced the ultimate danger of a two-front war.

The Franco-Russian alliance created two armed camps in Europe. Few realized the importance of this at the time. The Balkans were relatively quiet and Russia, busy with the trans-Siberian railway, was preoccupied in Asia. Russia's principal rival in Asia was still Britain. France also was in dispute with Britain over south-east Asia and parts of Africa. Germany therefore felt no immediate threat. Indeed by signing a new trading treaty with Russia in 1894 and by warning off Austria from adventures in the Balkans, German relations with Russia improved. Britain was the power with the most problems and by hinting about an Anglo-German alliance, William's ministers felt they had a commanding position in Europe.

Germany and Britain

Although both might feel themselves likely enemies of France and Russia, Germany and Britain found themselves quite unable to agree on military and naval matters or about colonies and trade. Russia's fears that Britain might join the Triple Alliance did not come true. From 1890 onwards relations between Germany and Britain grew worse. On a personal level there was growing unfriendliness between William and his grandmother, and his uncle, the Prince of Wales. Each year from 1889 to 1895 William came to the Isle of Wight for Cowes week.

'The Emperor's arrival was always impressive. When the imperial yacht *Hohenzollern* entered the harbour escorted by a group of German warships, the Royal Navy gave it a twenty-one gun salute and the hundreds of private craft lying in anchor, dipped their pennants. From then on there was an elaborate round of festivities; the Queen gave a state banquet at Osborne, the Prince entertained nightly at the Royal Yacht Club, Ger-

The *Hohenzollern* in Kiel Canal

man and British bands vied with each other to serenade the townspeople, the two navies exchanged a flow of hospitality and hostesses fought with each other to fill the gaps.'[1]

In 1891 William came on a full state visit with hundreds of followers. He brought his new yacht *Meteor*, which he insisted on keeping in a race even when the wind had dropped completely and so missed dinner with his grandmother. Queen Victoria began to find his visits increasingly tiresome, and the Prince of Wales was, at times, barely able to keep his temper in check.

More serious were the quarrels between the two powers in various parts of the world, mainly in Africa. On one occasion Germany sided with France to stop Britain giving Sudanese territory to the Congo. Germany offered to protect the Boer Republics (Transvaal and Orange Free State) which Cecil Rhodes, the Prime Minister of Cape Colony, wanted to take over. In December 1895, encouraged by Rhodes, Dr Jameson invaded Transvaal with a few hundred followers. Jameson hoped the British settlers would rise in rebellion. Instead he was quickly captured. William saw this as an opportunity to declare the Transvaal as a German Protectorate but his ministers warned him that this could lead to war with Britain. Instead he sent a telegram to President Kruger of Transvaal congratulating him

[1] Cowles, *The Kaiser*, p. 123.

on having kept the peace in the face of armed bands of invaders 'without having to call for help from friendly powers'. Few people in Britain had supported Jameson's action but the interference of the Kaiser caused a howl of rage. Officers of the 1st Royal Dragoons, of which William had been appointed Honorary Colonel-in-Chief, tore up his portrait and burnt the pieces. One British ambassador stated in 1914 that Anglo-German hostility began with the Kruger telegram in January 1896.

Britain was also becoming unhappy about the closer co-operation between Russia and Germany. Nicholas II became Tsar in 1894. This new co-operation was first shown in 1895, following the victory of Japan over China. Russia, France and Germany combined to force Japan to give up one of her prizes, the Liaotung Peninsula. William began talking of vast armies of Chinese and Japanese – 'the Yellow Peril' – marching on Europe. Russia and Germany, William told Nicholas II, must stand shoulder to shoulder to hold back this threat. While William may have believed in such a danger, he probably wanted to keep the Russians busy in Asia. Here they would come face to face with Japan and Britain. Otherwise Russia would turn back to the Balkans and might fight a war with Germany.

William's deepening interests in Africa and Asia in the late 1890s showed how far he was turning away from Bismarck's policies. The latter had made Germany the most powerful state on the continent of Europe and had been content with that position. William began to look beyond the bounds of Europe. Under pressure from merchants, industrialists, colonialists and admirals, all of whom believed Germany deserved, or would benefit from, a vast overseas empire, William sought to spread German power across the world. In 1897, after the murder of two German missionaries, the Chinese port of Kiaochow was taken over as a German base. In 1898 Germany secured from Spain the Caroline, the Pelew and the Marianne islands. In 1899 Britain agreed to Germany taking two of the Samoan Islands. Germany began to take over Britain's role as protector of the Ottoman Empire. Plans to build a railway from Constantinople to Bagdad, with German money and engineers, were announced in 1899.

The German Navy

Britain probably had no serious objections to Germany's taking over territories and islands across the globe. William, however, had long been certain that Germany could not be a world power, or even protect her colonies, without a great navy. He was fascinated by sailing and the sea. In 1889 he had been present at the annual review of the British fleet and had stared in amazement at the long rows of ironclads. In 1890 he set up the Imperial Naval Office. 'What William I had done for the Army', wrote one German Chancellor, 'William II wished to do for the Navy.' The Reichstag could see no reason to spend

Von Tirpitz

money on battleships. The German army, unwilling to see its own share of the Imperial revenue reduced, also opposed the 'Big Navy' policy.

In 1897 the Naval Estimates were actually cut by 12 million marks. William was infuriated by the behaviour of the Reichstag. He was determined to get his large navy even if he had to march the army into the Reichstag and disband it. Such a desperate course did not become necessary for the same year

William found the man who was to both convince Germany of the need for a big navy and to be the architect of the new fleet. The man was Alfred von Tirpitz, then aged forty-eight, a huge black-bearded sailor who had reached the rank of admiral. The first Naval Bill, laid before the Reichstag by Tirpitz, showed a change of heart. It was passed by 212 votes to 139 on 28 March 1898. This increased the number of battleships from 7 to 19, of heavy cruisers from 4 to 12 and of light cruisers from 7 to 30. Shortly afterwards the German Navy League was founded to convince the public of the need for a strong navy because Britain was very jealous of German progress (see chapter 9). To those who said that even an enlarged fleet would be no match for Britain, Tirpitz replied that before being destroyed the German fleet would deal a mortal blow. Therefore Britain would not risk an attack. The Navy League grew rapidly in size and influence, enrolling a million members by 1906. Few Germans objected to further Naval Bills proposing bigger fleets.

Britain was not very worried by Germany's early naval increases. She aimed to have a navy as strong as any other two powers and Germany's was only seventh in size. In 1896 Britain had possessed 33 battleships to Germany's 6 and 130 heavy cruisers to Germany's 4. By 1900 Britain had other more pressing problems. Most of her army and an increasing number of troops from her Empire were fighting in South Africa against the Boers. There were bitter quarrels with France over territories in North Africa, and with Russia, which was taking over the Chinese province of Manchuria. Since Germany also opposed Russia's policy in China both she and Britain had a common link. The British Colonial Secretary, Joseph Chamberlain, used this understanding to begin talks with German diplomats about the possibility of an alliance between the two countries.

Between 1898 and 1901 discussions took place, without result. Firstly Britain's war against the Boers made her very unpopular especially in Germany. When Joseph Chamberlain, in a speech at Leicester in November 1899, referred to Germany as Britain's 'natural ally' there were loud protests in Germany. Secondly there was the old problem of Germany's position in Europe and the fact that the Royal Navy could not help in a land war. Germany had no wish to fight Russia and France to save Britain's colonies. Finally the two countries could not agree about the terms of an alliance. Britain merely wanted a defensive alliance in case either side was attacked by two or more powers. Germany wanted Britain to become a full member of the Triple Alliance so that she would become involved in any of the alliance's wars.

The greatest possibility of an alliance came early in 1901 when William abandoned his duties in Germany to hurry to the bedside of his dying grandmother, Queen Victoria. Public opinion in Britain swung behind William but strong opposition from the German government ended any hopes. By the end of 1901 *The Times* was commenting that 'these daily manifestations of German hatred, which at first caused surprise rather than hatred, are gradually sinking into the hearts of the British people'. By this time any possibility of an alliance with Germany had been abandoned by British politicians.

Britain looked elsewhere for her security. In 1901 a treaty with the USA allowed Britain to reduce her navy in the Caribbean and concentrate more on home defence. The following year the Anglo-Japanese Alliance barred the Russian advance into East Asia and more British ships were returned to Europe.

Thus Britain had moved away from her dangerous isolation, while Germany no longer held the balance among France and Russia and Britain. After 1900 Italy began to shake free of the Triple Alliance leaving Germany and her unstable ally, Austria-Hungary, as the isolated powers.

9 William and Germany 1890–1914

The Kaiser

The fall of Bismarck in 1890 clearly meant that, unlike his grandfather, William II was determined to show that he was the real ruler of Germany. This was not surprising since William regarded himself as 'the instrument' of God and once referred to the Almighty as 'Our Old Ally'. At the royal court William was referred to (at least in his hearing) by titles such as 'the Most High'. His personal letters were sent in blue envelopes on which was written 'Expressed by the order of the All Highest'. As the powerful ruler of more than 50 million subjects William naturally lived and moved about in great splendour. Throughout Germany he owned more than thirty houses, castles and palaces and in 1888–90 had many redecorated at great cost. He travelled across Europe in a specially built cream-and-gold royal train. It had twelve coaches for the many courtiers and officers who always accompanied him. William's saloon car was upholstered in blue satin. For more distant journeys William was provided with a steam yacht, the *Hohenzollern*.

Most people quickly recognized the new Kaiser by his up-turned moustache, lovingly tended every morning at seven by the court barber. By comparison with the great bulk of Bismarck, William was small, 1·77 metres tall and weighing less than 70 kg. He showed little interest in food, a fact which caused some grumbling among his dinner guests. He drank heavily only on rare occasions, but enjoyed an occasional cigarette. His useless left arm did not appear to embarrass him. He was a good shot and a skilled horseman and, as those who shook his hand found to their cost, he developed great strength in his right arm and grip. Throughout most of his life William enjoyed good health and indeed lived to be eighty-two. Most of his waking life he wore uniform and expected his courtiers and officials to do the same – often in outfits he had personally designed. He particularly enjoyed collecting foreign uniforms,

Austrian, British and Russian, which he exchanged for German ones. He changed his clothes to suit the occasion. It was said that he wore the uniform of an Admiral of the Fleet to visit an aquarium and that of a General of the Engineers to the dinner of the Berlin Motor Club.

By 1892 after eleven years of marriage, William was the father of six sons and one daughter, Victoria Louise. He treated the boys with harsh discipline and was unwilling to listen to them. The eldest son, also named William, was no credit to his father's upbringing. He gained a reputation for wild living, whilst the fourth son, August Wilhelm, eventually became a Nazi storm-trooper and SS *Gruppenführer*. The fifth son, Oscar, also joined the Nazi Party. William's wife, the Empress Augusta Victoria, known in the royal family as Dona, was a loving, obedient but rather dull woman. In many ways she was the ideal partner for the unstable Kaiser. She was utterly devoted to him and understood his weaknesses but, unlike his mother, had no strong views of her own on politics. William found her company boring for long periods. Dona's main interests were battling against vice and immorality at court and in Berlin and raising money to build churches, of which she helped to found forty-two.

The shadow of his righteous wife hung over William. Unlike his uncle Edward VII, William did not chase pretty women, although he certainly enjoyed their company and their flattery. More sinister hints, without any foundation, were whispered against William's long friendship with Count Philip Eulenberg. In 1908 Eulenberg, a happily married man and father of eight children, was charged with perjury during a libel case relating to talk of serious immorality. The charge and trial which followed destroyed Eulenberg's health and the case was indefinitely adjourned. William made no move to defend Eulenberg.

William, then, lacked both a happy home life and major political successes. These failures helped to produce mental and physical tensions which showed up in two main ways. Firstly, William was extremely restless and earned the nickname of *Reisekaiser* (the travelling Kaiser). Among his longer journeys were twelve visits to Britain between 1889 and 1911, visits to Italy in 1893, Russia in 1897, the Holy Land in 1898 and

Morocco in 1905. He made frequent trips to Austria, both to see the Emperor Francis-Joseph and to indulge in his favourite sport of shooting. Each June he attended the Kiel Regatta which he followed by a cruise in the Baltic. In July the untiring Emperor took a party of selected guests up the coast of Norway, ordering them to do physical exercises on deck before breakfast. Even elderly admirals were not excused. August found him at his castle of Wilhelmshöhe near his schooldays' city of Kassel. Here he went riding at 6.30 a.m., played tennis, took long hikes through the forests and dug out the Roman ruins in the area. Naturally those courtiers who were unfortunate enough to go with him had to take part in all these strenuous activities. In September and November William moved on to other places. In between these tiring journeys he also found time for weekend trips, steaming across Germany in the royal train. One Berlin newspaper calculated that between August 1893 and August 1894 William spent 199 days travelling!

Secondly, in between his journeys William enjoyed public occasions at which he usually made a speech. He first spoke in public at the Cologne Carnival of 1877 when he was eighteen. Once on the throne he could not be silenced. During the first ten years of his reign he made over 400 speeches – approximately one every ten days. His language was intended to stir its hearers but it was old-fashioned rather than dramatic. This was clearly shown in his address to troops leaving Germany in 1900 to suppress the Boxer Uprising in China. 'Live up to Prussia's traditional steadfastness,' he said, 'show yourselves Christians, happily enduring in the face of heathens. May honour and fame attend your colours and arms. Give the world an example of virility and discipline. . . . Carry yourselves like men and may the blessing of God go with you.' William's speeches greatly offended many Germans, especially the rapidly growing Socialist Party. He once told army recruits that one day they might have to fire on their own families.

Over many years William's constant travelling, hasty speeches and interference in government made him increasingly unpopular both in Germany and abroad. As early as 1894 Professor Ludwig Quidde published a book, *Caligula or a Study in Caesarian Madness*. It drew a brilliant parallel between Rome during the reign of the insane Emperor Caligula and contemporary Germany, without of course, mentioning the latter country. The men who surrounded William never told him of his unpopularity. On the contrary, politicians, generals and admirals hurried to carry out his orders. Indeed they protected him, as far as possible, from the truths of the outside world by accepting his opinions and censoring his reading matters, especially newspapers. But they could not hide unsatisfactory votes in the Reichstag or diplomatic failures abroad. William did not hide his anger against those who spoilt his plans. He told the Reichstag that it was the army and not they who had welded together the Empire. Social Democrats, he said, were enemies of himself and of Germany. When the occasion demanded it he had similar harsh words for the British, the French, the Japanese and the Russians.

By the standards of 1900 William was not a racialist. He often spoke of the 'yellow peril' – armies of Chinese and Japanese invading Europe – but he also said 'Never forget that though people . . . have skins of a different colour, they for all that possess hearts susceptible to feelings of honour. Handle such people gently.' William had no visions of conquering the world like an Attila or a Genghis Khan. He was painfully aware that the German Empire was less than a generation old when he became Emperor. He looked at the enormous British Empire protected by its navy, and at the rapidly growing strength of the USA, Russia and Japan. He probably thought that unless he made a determined effort to make Germany a world power, his Empire would then decline like Austria and Turkey.

William and the Politicians

For more than twenty-seven years Bismarck had been the principal minister, first of Prussia and then of the German Empire. During the twenty-seven years following his fall, four men served as Imperial Chancellor: General Georg Caprivi (1890–94), Prince Chlodwig Hohenlöhe-Shillingsfurst (1894–1900), Prince Bernhard von Bulow (1900–09) and Theodore Bethmann-Hollweg (1909–17). None of these four could remotely compare with Bismarck in political skill or foreign diplomacy. More seriously for Germany, none was able to create a working partnership with William II similar to that which had existed between William I and Bismarck. Through-

Von Bülow

out this period whilst William II was undermining his own authority, his Chancellors, battling with increasing problems both at home and abroad, were losing power. By 1914 the Reichstag was enjoying much greater authority than ever it had done under Bismarck.

In his bid to become popular with all classes in Germany, William's reign began with a number of progressive measures. The persecution of the Socialist Party ended in September 1890 and social reforms were made. Factory inspectors were given greater powers, and the hours of work of women and children limited. Import duties on food were heavily cut. Army service was reduced from three years to two. William tried to cut down the political power of the Junkers in Prussia. The great landowners were particularly upset by this attack on their powers and their income (through foreign food imports). In 1893 the Landowners' League was formed to fight the Kaiser's policies.

A far more serious threat appeared to all those with property and power in Germany with the rapid growth of the Socialist Party. At the Erfurt Congress in 1891 the Socialists decided to follow Marx's ideas of violent revolution and class warfare. Between 1890 and 1903 the Socialists increased their seats in the Reichstag from 35 to 81, and in 1912 they became the largest party, with 110 seats. William became worried by the growth of Socialism. When in the 1890s Anarchist bomb attacks began to threaten Europe's heads of state, he decided to act. In September 1894, after the assassination of President Carnot of France, William called on the Conservatives to rally to him: 'Forward into battle for religion, for morality and for order against the parties of revolution.' He tried twice to have an anti-Socialist Bill reintroduced, but in vain.

The threat of Socialism did, however, draw the right-wing Conservative groups together, especially the great industrialists and the Junkers; the alliance of 'steel and rye'. The leader of this grouping was Baron von Stumm-Halberg, a Saar steel-master, who ran his works like a military camp. William was pressed to use the army to seize full power himself by reducing or abolishing the powers of the Reichstag. In 1894, 1897 and 1899 it appeared that he might take this drastic step but each time he hesitated. Thus from 1894 onwards William gave up his attempts to gain popularity and concentrated on saving the monarchy and its supporters. Laws were passed to curb the effective powers of the Socialist parties and trade unions.

A further blow for the industrial workers came in 1902, when Germany reimposed high tariffs on imported food and manufactured goods. This increased prices at a time when the cost of living was already rising. This in turn led to demands for wage increases and with the Socialist Party working closely with the trade unions instead of plotting revolution, the industrial workers were united. So also were the employers. Between 1898 and 1900, 114 employers' associations were founded. They set up in a central anti-strike bureau. Therefore, Germany became the centre of some of Europe's bitterest industrialist disputes before 1914.

William naturally sided with the employers against the Socialist-led unions. The government tried to ease the pressure by further social reforms, this time with the co-operation of most political parties, including the Socialists. The strikes continued but mostly failed against the wealthy employers' associations. Instead the trade union–Socialist alliance made political demands. In 1905 vast parades of workers marched through Germany's major cities demanding votes for all men and secret ballots in local State elections. They were successful in Baden, Bavaria and Württemberg, but the main problem was Prussia. The system of voting there was so organized that in 1908 the Socialists gained 23 per cent of the votes but only 7 seats, whilst the Conservatives with 16 per cent of the votes gained 212 seats. As a result of angry demonstrations, William promised reform, but nothing was done. Indeed Bethmann-Hollweg proposed changes which would have strengthened the Conservatives.

There were more strikes and demonstrations in 1910 and in the Reichstag elections of January 1912 the Socialists and left-wing Liberals campaigned strongly against the Conservatives. The result gave the Socialists 110 seats, the left Liberals 42, and the Centre 91.

It is clear that after 1900 the Emperor, the Chancellors and the people who supported them, such as the Junkers and the Navy League, were under pressure. This pressure came from political parties of the centre and left. Political and social reforms were won and, but for the outbreak of war, Germany might have moved very close to becoming a 'constitutional monarchy' like Britain. The parties which did so well in the 1912 election were unfortunately still very divided among themselves. The establishment of a genuine parliamentary democracy still had far to go in Germany. This was shown in 1913 at Zabern in Alsace. A young officer of an infantry regiment stationed in the town made offensive remarks about the local inhabitants. Demonstrations followed, the troops were brought out and twenty-eight civilians, including a judge, were thrown into military cells. This was illegal, and by a large majority the Reichstag condemned the government for supporting the army's action. William's reply was to decorate the Commanding Officer at Zabern. But when war broke out in August 1914, even the Socialists justified their support for the Emperor and the unpopular army on the grounds that it was a fight against Tsarist oppression. A party truce was called and there were no more political reforms for four years.

Economic Developments

Under William II Germany continued to develop economically until by 1914 she was, apart from the USA, the world's leading industrial power. Between 1890 and 1914 German industry increased production threefold. By comparison there was only a two-fifths increase in Britain. By the latter date also Germany had a larger population than any country in Europe apart from Russia. The 50 million population of 1890 had grown to 67 million by 1914. By comparison the population of France increased by a mere 3 million between 1870 and 1914. In Germany the growth of towns and cities such as Berlin and Essen was quite dramatic. The agricultural population remained the same at 25 million. By 1914 more than 60 per cent of Germans lived in towns, compared with only 40 per cent in 1890.

The number of people working in manufacturing industries, transport trade and the professions, therefore, grew rapidly during the reign of William II. One of the most rapidly growing industries at this time, as also in Britain and the USA, was coal. The number of miners tripled to over 700,000 as did production, which reached 279 million tons in 1913, almost equalling British output. The great centre of mining was in the Ruhr. From there came 60 per cent of Germany's coal; from Silesia 14 per cent and from the Saar about 4 per cent. Nearly one-third of all Germany's coal still went into the furnaces of her booming metallurgical industries. The growth of the German steel industry, also centred in the Ruhr, was remarkable. Between 1890 and 1900 output more than tripled from 2·2 million tons to 6·7 million, making Germany the largest steel producer in Europe. Between 1900 and 1913 production almost tripled again to 18·9 million tons. Only the vast works of the USA, with 31·8 million tons, produced more. Britain, which had led the world in 1870, was only third by 1913 with slightly under 7 million tons. Much of Germany's growing steel production was used by her shipbuilding industry. By 1913 with over 3 million tons of shipping, Germany was easily the second major sea power after Britain. The German Navy also expanded greatly during William's reign. Railway building continued after 1890 increasing 50 per cent in length to reach 63,000 kilometres in 1913. Only the vast Russian Empire had a larger rail system in Europe.

Berlin overhead railway accident

Germany had most of the equipment for economic growth and prosperity; a growing and well-educated labour force; money for capital investment; ample fuel supplies; excellent rail and waterways and steel, the basic material of industry and technology. As mentioned on p. 64 it was Germany's achievements in the advanced scientific industries (chemicals, electricals, machinery and machine tools, and after 1890, motor vehicles) which made her a rival of the USA. By 1900 Germany had passed Britain as an advanced industrial nation.

Germany's heavy chemical industry was based on her use of pyrites, common salt and crude potassium salts. Output of the

118

last named rose from 1·3 million tons in 1891 to 9·7 in 1911. Heavy chemicals, which employed 45,000 persons in 1907, were used in manufacturing and for agricultural fertilizers. Exports of chemicals more than doubled between 1895 and 1910. Germany's lead in producing dyestuffs was enormous. By 1913 Germany accounted for 90 per cent of the world's exports of dyestuffs worth some £10 million. The electrical industry grew most quickly in the Rhine valley, where generators could be powered by waste hot gases from the Ruhr steelworks. The production of electrical energy in this area grew 150-fold between 1901 and 1915. The number of workers in the electrical industry grew from 25,000 to 107,000 between 1895 and 1906. By 1913 production of electrical goods in Germany was worth £65 million, of which £11 million worth was exported. Britain and the USA exported only £8 million worth together. The German machine-tool industry owed its success to the American example. As early as 1899 Loewe of Berlin rebuilt his works on American lines and used American inventions. The Wolf machine works at Madgeburg was also a pioneer of this industry. Compared with steel, chemicals and electricals the German motor industry was insignificant until the 1930s. However, one merely has to remember the names of Daimler, Diesel, Benz (and his daughter Mercedes) to realize the important developments made in Germany in the motor industry, and the name of Zeppelin in aviation.

As production increased so the number of companies engaged grew fewer in number and much larger in size. Two great firms, Siemens and AEG, dominated the electrical industry and by 1916 chemical manufacturing was almost a monopoly. In coal, steel and heavy engineering cartels (see p. 63) continued to increase. The Rhenish-Westphalian Coal Syndicate formed in 1893 controlled half Germany's output of coal and coke. The Steel Union was formed in 1904 and by 1911 included thirty large steel works, one of which was Krupps. Each steel firm concentrated on a small range of goods and brought raw materials and fuel and sold its products at fixed prices. The number of industrial cartels rose from 70 in 1887 to 300 by 1900 and 600 in 1911. By the last date therefore, every important industry had its cartel.

As population and production grew overseas trade became

increasingly important to Germany. Food, raw materials and particular types of manufactured goods had to be imported. To pay for these Germany sold abroad chemicals, metal goods and machinery, textiles and coal. In 1890 Germany was buying nearly £200 million worth of foreign goods and selling goods worth £153 million. By 1913 imports had risen to £526 million and exports to £495 million. German merchants penetrated the markets of North and South America, Africa and Asia. Like Britain, Germany suffered a 'trade gap', but more than made up the difference by dividends from foreign investments worth over £1,000 million and her earnings from shipping and banking.

Before 1914 the German worker was the best protected in the world from the effects of sickness, accident and old age. Otherwise, working conditions were less pleasant than in the other two leading industrial countries, Britain and the USA. The average German worked nearly two hours per day longer than his British counterpart in 1890. Even by 1912 the average German working day was longer than the average British had been in 1877. Despite the longer working day, German workers earned nearly one-third less than workers in Britain. The outbreak of World War I inevitably reduced living standards, creating great unrest.

10 The Isolation of Germany 1900–1914

The Entente Cordiale

William was very pleased to hear of the Anglo-Japanese Alliance in 1902 for Japan appeared to be heading for a clash with Russia. This in turn, perhaps, would lead to war between Britain and Russia thereby involving France. This would leave Germany in a strong bargaining position. William strongly encouraged Nicholas II's ambitions in the Far East, referring to him as 'Admiral of the Pacific'. Relations between Germany and Britain were still uncertain. William got on much more happily with the new Prince of Wales (later George V), but he was not at all pleased to hear about Anglo-French talks and Edward VII's visit to Paris. Feelings between Britain and France were still bitter in 1903 and Edward was greeted by boos when he arrived in Paris. For three days he waved and smiled, praising everything about France and the French and was loudly cheered when he left for home. William reacted by reminding the French of Napoleon I and warning them of British treachery. He also warned Russia that the Crimean coalition (Britain and France) was being revived.

Russia soon had more real problems to face when the Japanese fleet attacked her ships at Port Arthur in February 1904. As France was the ally of Russia and Britain of Japan, William felt that the danger of an Anglo-French understanding was past. He was quite mistaken. Within two months Britain and France had signed an agreement, the *Entente Cordiale*, settling their disputes in Asia, Africa and North America. It was not a military alliance but it ended any possibility of an Anglo-French clash in distant waters. This was important because by 1904 Britain clearly realised that the German fleet was a direct menace.

William's hopes that Britain and France would be dragged into the Russo-Japanese war, thus destroying either the Franco-Russian or the Anglo-French agreement, was soon lost.

Surprisingly Russia was no match for Japan either on land or at sea. Early in 1905 Russia's armies were defeated at Mukden in a fourteen-day battle, and her Baltic fleet almost completely sunk at Tsushima. William did what he could to help Russia by providing coaling ships for her fleet but he dare not risk joining the fighting. This would have automatically brought in Britain, who would have destroyed Germany's fleet and overseas empire. However, William's advisers realized that, with Russia reeling and France without another military ally, an opportunity had opened for Germany.

At the Tsar's suggestion William had had a draft treaty drawn up by which Russia, Germany and France would unite to deal with the Anglo-Japanese alliance. Nicholas refused to sign it unless the French were first consulted. William dare not allow this to happen for fear of bringing down the sudden wrath of the Royal Navy on Germany. Fear of a British naval strike on the growing fleet haunted William and his advisers in 1904. Instead they decided to show France how worthless were her alliance with the beaten Russians and her *Entente* with Britain in the face of Germany's massed armies.

Morocco 1905

The German government chose the future of Morocco as the issue with which to bring the French to heel. The *Entente* of April 1904 with Britain had stated that Morocco was to be an area where France was to have the major role. In February 1905 the French began to put pressure on the Sultan to grant various privileges. The Germans claimed quite rightly that by the Treaty of Madrid of 1880 they and all the other signatories should be consulted before any changes were made. The Germans also hoped to establish a naval base and possibly to find iron ore deposits in Morocco. In the spring of 1905 William took his court and members of the government on a Mediterranean cruise in the liner *Hamburg*. He was persuaded, against his will, to pay a courtesy call on the Sultan in Tangier. He realised such an action would be seen as a direct challenge to Britain and, especially, France. A heavy sea was running as the *Hamburg* dropped anchor in Tangier harbour. Not until an officer, dressed in cavalry uniform with spurs, had made a trial run, did William agree to go ashore. Then to his dismay he had to ride a frisky white stallion through the narrow streets, 'crowded with anarchists'. The visit to the Sultan lasted only three hours but it was long enough for the Germans to encourage the Sultan to resist French demands.

After the Kaiser's visit the German government called for an international conference on Morocco. Delcassé, the French Foreign Minister, pleaded with his government to resist, even when hints were dropped of a German attack in western Europe. The French, possibly remembering 1870, were not prepared to face such a threat and agreed to a conference. Delcassé resigned.

William's visit to Tangiers

Björkö

William was delighted by the French retreat. In July 1905 he prepared for the next stage in the creation of a 'continental league'. He was taking his annual cruise in the Northern Seas and casually cabled the Tsar to meet him. Nicholas suggested the Bay of Björkö in Finland. The Tsar was still deeply depressed by the almost complete loss of his fleet at Tsushima in May. William thought he could now detach Russia from France. On the deck of his yacht *Hohenzollern*, both made fierce attacks on Edward VII and Britain. Then William suggested that Russia and Germany should sign a treaty to help each other if attacked by a third European power. He showed a draft of the treaty to Nicholas who read it through three times and said 'That is excellent. I agree.' He then signed it. 'Tears of pure joy filled my eyes,' wrote William, 'for by God's grace the morning of 24th July 1905 at Björkö has witnessed the turning-point in the history of Europe; a great load has been lifted from my dear Fatherland which has finally escaped from the terrible Franco-Russian pincers.'

Unfortunately for William the Björkö treaty proved to be a complete failure. The German Foreign Minister regarded it as valueless because it excluded action in Asia. He even threatened resignation. The Russian government was even more astonished by its Emperor and in due course Nicholas had to tell William that 'Björkö' was a dead letter. Russia obviously could not promise to come to the assistance of both Germany and France, especially if the last two were fighting each other. The Russian government preferred to remain loyal to the 1894 Alliance with France.

Algeciras 1906

The collapse of the Björkö Treaty was a great disappointment to William, but he still hoped to create a continental league. He and his advisers looked to the coming international conference on Morocco but there were two sets of ideas about this. William hoped to woo the French away from Britain. Others thought that France would be convinced only if the threat of the German army was shown to be greater than the protection of the Royal Navy. Although William never intended a war against France over Morocco, two important military decisions were made at this time. In December 1905 General Alfred von Schlieffen, Chief of the German General Staff, produced his strategic plan for invading France through Holland and Belgium. In the same month a new Liberal government was elected in Britain and began highly secret military discussions with France which went on until 1914.

The Moroccan Conference was held from January to April 1906 in the Spanish port of Algeciras, close to Gibraltar. All the major European powers, as well as several minor ones, were represented; so also were the USA and Morocco itself. The German delegation found that very few others supported it. Britain and France stood firm and Russia, in need of a loan, supported the latter; Spain and Italy were conscious of British naval power while the USA did not fully understand the issues. When a vote was taken on a minor issue only Morocco and Austria-Hungary supported Germany. The other seven powers ranged solidly against her. This led to a softening of Germany's tough approach. Nevertheless as a result of the Conference France was left as the major power in Morocco. Germany was given some minor powers but most importantly the Anglo-French *Entente* had been reinforced. When the opportunity to take sides had occurred Germany found that she could count only upon her unstable ally of twenty-seven years standing, Austria-Hungary. William II and his government were unhappily aware that Russia had twice in recent months failed to enter the German camp. Even Italy, the third member of the Triple Alliance, had shown herself to be a most doubtful friend.

Russia and Britain

Germany's growing isolation was increased by the Anglo-Russian *Entente* signed in 1907. Like the Anglo-French *Entente* of 1904 this was no military alliance. The agreement merely set out to remove British and Russian differences in colonial matters, particularly in Persia. However, until at least 1904, William had always assumed that Britain's disputes with Russia and France were too serious ever to be settled except by war. Germany's armed might could then be used to tip the balance either way, thus giving her enormous bargaining power. During the years 1902–07 this policy had collapsed. Britain had made an alliance with Japan, a firm understanding with France and an agreement with France's ally, Russia. William had meanwhile seen the failure of his attempts to link first with Russia and then with France. By 1907 the German press was beginning to talk of the 'ring' closing round Germany.

Even more serious was the growing ill-feeling between Britain and Germany after 1906. In that year Britain launched the first Dreadnought battleship. This class of warship carried ten large guns instead of the usual four and was also faster than any previous battleship. The decision to build Dreadnoughts had been made in 1904 by the British Government on the advice of the First Sea Lord, Sir John Fisher. Britain did not believe that Germany would have the skill, the shipyards or the money to build similar ships. By 1907 in fact, the first German Dreadnought had been launched, with plans to launch four more each year from 1908 to 1911. Britain's own plans to build twenty Dreadnoughts during these four years, were not now thought to be sufficient to protect her shores. As the British Government was also planning to introduce social services such as old age pensions and labour exchanges it did not want an expensive naval arms race with Germany. It was suggested that the two powers should limit their building. Not only were William and his ministers, especially Tirpitz, opposed to a 'naval holiday' but so also were the majority of the Reichstag and the leaders of German industry. Only a solemn promise by Britain to remain neutral in a European war would have been sufficient to achieve limitation. This would have driven France and Russia into an alliance with Germany, out of fear that Britain would join the Triple Alliance.

The most important single feature of the Dreadnought was that it made all other battleships out of date. Britain had almost lost her naval superiority overnight unless she could remain ahead of Germany in building Dreadnoughts. Fears of a German invasion were very strong in 1908 and a popular cry was 'we want eight, and we won't wait'. In 1909 the Government did announce its intention to build eight Dreadnoughts at once and to try to keep a 3 to 2 lead over Germany.

William certainly had no plans to invade Britain in 1908, but his attempts to improve the position merely made things worse. In February he took the unusual step of writing a private letter to Lord Tweedsmuir, the First Lord of the Admiralty. William

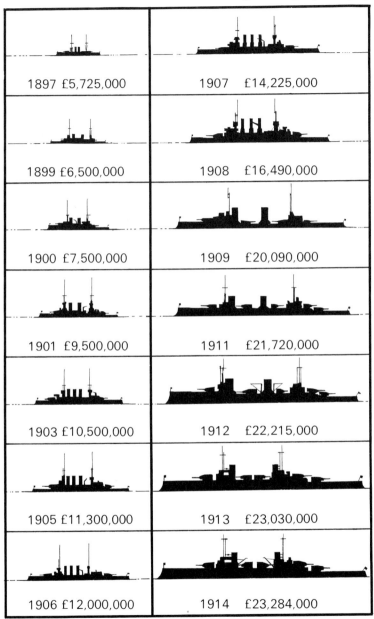

1897 £5,725,000

1907 £14,225,000

1899 £6,500,000

1908 £16,490,000

1900 £7,500,000

1909 £20,090,000

1901 £9,500,000

1911 £21,720,000

1903 £10,500,000

1912 £22,215,000

1905 £11,300,000

1913 £23,030,000

1906 £12,000,000

1914 £23,284,000

Annual expenditure on the German Navy

tried to show that the German fleet was no threat to Britain. 'This perpetual quoting of the "German Danger"', he wrote, 'is utterly unworthy of the great British nation with its world-wide Empire and its mighty navy which is about five times the size of the German navy. There is something ludicrous about it. . . .' No-one in Britain thought that William's letter was helpful. Indeed Edward VII wrote a mild reprimand to him. In October 1908 William gave an interview, which was published in the *Daily Telegraph*, complaining of his poor 'press' in Britain and the ingratitude shown to him during the Boer War, when despite Russia's attempts to form a 'continental league' he had remained neutral. William also harped back to the 'yellow peril' and the need to 'deal' with Japan. The publication of this article brought angry comments from Russia, from France, from Japan and from within Germany itself where the fight of the Boers had been applauded. British readers did not welcome being called 'mad as March hares' or being told that most Germans 'hated them'.

At the same time, Germany was very worried about a 'Copenhagen attack' by the British fleet before their own was large enough to resist fully.[1] Although the Kiel Canal linking the Baltic to the North Sea had been widened to take Dreadnoughts the docks of north-west Germany could hold only twelve battleships. The rest of Germany's large warships were therefore forced to remain in the Baltic. Britain had meanwhile concentrated the bulk of her Grand Fleet in the North Sea. Also it was no secret that Sir John Fisher had long favoured an attack on Germany, especially after 1907.

Thus ill-feeling between the two countries grew rapidly. The main feeling in Germany was that Britain could be kept at bay only by threats, a policy which had failed with France over Morocco. British opinion was becoming convinced that Germany, secure on the continent with her large well-equipped army, was determined to become the world's greatest naval power. This navy would then be used to conquer the British Empire and take over its trade.

---

[1] In 1807 the British Fleet captured the ships of neutral Denmark to prevent Napoleon I seizing them.

The Balkans 1908

The worsening of Anglo-German relations was followed quickly by a Russo-German split. As in Bismarck's time the scene of the quarrel was in the Balkans. Russia's defeat by Japan in 1904–05 had ended her Far East ambitions and reawakened her interest in south-east Europe. Although in 1897 Russia and Austria had signed an agreement to keep the situation stable in the Balkans, their co-operation had steadily broken down. In 1903 Alexander, the pro-Austrian King of Serbia, and his queen were murdered by army officers. A supporter of Russia, Peter Karageorgevic, took his place on the throne. Since Serbia was the leading Pan-Slav nation, dedicated to freeing the Slavs from Austrian rule, Austro-Serbian relations became 'poisonous'. Austria banned agricultural and livestock imports from Serbia – the so-called 'pig war' – in an attempt to weaken the latter's economy. In 1906 a new Austrian Foreign Minister, Count von Aehrenthal, was appointed, determined to strengthen the Empire's position. In the same year Prince Alexander Isvolsky, who was very interested in the Pan-Slav movement and Russia's role in the Balkans, became the Tsar's Foreign Minister. The two men met frequently in a bid to settle their differences without giving away too much. By 1908 they had provisionally agreed that Russian warships should be allowed to pass through the Straits. In return Russia would allow Austria to add to her Empire the Turkish provinces of Bosnia and Herzegovina which she (Austria) had occupied since 1878.

In July 1908 a revolution broke out in Turkey. Austria took advantage of the situation to arrange for Bulgaria, a rival of Serbia, to declare its complete independence. At the same time, Austria secretly annexed Bosnia and Herzegovina. These two moves infuriated Serbia and its ally, Russia, which had failed to gain its share of the bargain, the opening of the Straits. William II was enraged that Austria had not told him of her move. He called 'the annexation 'a robbery' and accused Vienna of 'duping us in the most unheard of fashion'.

In the Balkans tensions between Austria and Serbia mounted and threatened war, involving Russia. Russia, still recovering from her defeat by Japan, was in no condition to fight a major war. The German government began to put pressure on her to accept the new situation. Unable to face the prospect of a

German invasion, Russia reluctantly gave way.

The Balkans crisis of 1908 was a diplomatic victory for Germany but at the price of enormous Russian ill-feeling. It had also made Russia realize that she must work more closely with Britain and France. In the Balkans bitterness had grown between the Slavs and the Austrians. Bismarck's policy of holding Austria in check in this part of Europe had collapsed. Not only had Germany become closely involved with Turkey through railway building, but she had allowed herself to be dragged along behind Austria. It was because Germany had no friends among the other major powers that she felt the need to cling to Austria at any price. Thus by 1910 Germany found herself faced by three powerful and unfriendly nations, Britain, France and Russia, and chained to an ally who engaged in dangerous adventures.

The Path to War

William came to London in May 1910 for the funeral of his uncle Edward VII. Despite the unfriendly feelings between Germany and Britain and the personal dislike which had existed between Edward and himself, William was strongly attached to the British royal family. He genuinely mourned the passing of the king and his obvious grief awoke the sympathy of those who saw him. Whenever he appeared on the streets of Windsor or London he was warmly greeted by the crowds. This did not disguise the fact that the naval question could not be settled and that it was driving the two powers further apart.

In April 1911 Britain and Germany again confronted each other when the Moroccan problem reappeared. The Sultan of Morocco was faced by widespread revolts which he could not control and asked France for military help. William was on holiday on a Mediterranean island when the news reached him. 'It will suit us very well if the French commit themselves thoroughly with troops and money', he telegraphed the German Foreign Office, 'and in my opinion it is not in our interest to hinder them.' He also warned not to dispatch a gunboat to Tangier.

The new Foreign Secretary Kiderlen saw the chance to put pressure on France, for it was well known that the other two members of the *Entente*, Russia and Britain, were beginning to

The *Panther*

quarrel again in Asia. Kiderlen suggested that Germany should demand large compensations in Central Africa in return for giving France a free hand in Morocco. William expected the British to oppose this plan, but he was shortly to visit London for the unveiling of the Queen Victoria memorial. He therefore decided to discuss the matter with the new king, George V. The friendly reception and vague answers he received from George V evidently convinced William that the British government would not object to France's being bullied. On 1 July 1911 a German gunboat, the *Panther*, with 150 men arrived off the port of Agadir to 'protect' Germans living there. Some days later the German government announced that in return for recognizing French control of Morocco it wanted the French Congo, a vast colony in Central Africa.

The British government, in the person of the Chancellor of the Exchequer, David Lloyd George, warned Germany that no changes should be made without consulting Britain first. Lloyd George hinted that otherwise Britain would fight. The fleet prepared for action and the Chief of Staff, General Wilson, visited Paris with plans for bringing 170,000 troops to fight in France under French command. William was alarmed by the international storm and ordered his ministers to make smaller demands on France. By November Germany agreed to recognize French claims to Morocco and received 700,000 square kilometres of jungle in the French Congo in return.

William was even more unpopular at home after the *Panther* incident than he had been in 1908. 'Have we become a generation of women?' asked *Der Post*. Admiral Tirpitz used the affair as an excuse to ask for more money for warships. William was again persuaded that only by the threat of a large German navy could Britain be made to listen to him. Certainly Britain had not been happy at the prospect of a major war to save a French colony. Through the offer of the German shipping owner, Albert Ballin, the British War Minister Lord Haldane went to Berlin in 1912 in what was to be the last attempt to stop the 'battleship race'. There were too many powerful men in both countries not prepared to yield an inch. Essentially the mission failed because Germany still wanted Britain to promise that she would never take part in a European War. Only then was Germany prepared to limit or halt naval building. If Britain had given such a guarantee France or Russia, eventually both, would have been forced out of fear to side with Germany.

Instead Britain came to an arrangement with France in 1912 which virtually created a military alliance. Britain moved her heavy ships from the Mediterranean to the North Sea promising to protect the northern French coast. France moved her Atlantic squadrons into the Mediterranean, taking responsibility for British interests there. On hearing this news the Reichstag immediately voted more money for warships, which Tirpitz had asked for before Haldane's arrival.

Trouble soon spread to the Balkans. Italy, jealous of the French success in Morocco, landed troops in Turkey's North African province of Tripoli in September 1911. Italy and Turkey were soon fighting in the Straits, naturally worrying Russia. Italy's mediocre success against Turkey decided the smaller Balkan countries to act. Four of these countries – Serbia, Greece, Bulgaria and Montenegro – formerly ruled by Turkey, had formed the Balkans League. In October 1912 they attacked Turkey and overran almost all its remaining territories in Europe. Serbia, a land-locked country, announced that it intended to annexe Albania in order to give itself a coastline (see map on p. 68). Austria-Hungary immediately became alarmed in case Serbia eventually grew large enough to lead the Balkan League against Vienna. Led by General Conrad, the Chief of Staff in Austria, one important group called for war on Serbia. William II, alarmed at the prospect of a general war over Serbia, warned off Austria. Russia, worried that the unfriendly Bulgarians might get control of the Straits, warned off the League.

The Balkan war of 1912 was thus prevented from spreading. In June 1913 the victors fell out among themselves but the great powers arranged a peace conference. Serbia was again on the winning side, while Bulgaria lost all its gains. This naturally pleased Russia which disliked Bulgaria, and infuriated Austria which disliked Serbia. Serbia, however, had left some troops in northern Albania, and Austria, for the first time since 1908, acted decisively. Serbia was given eight days to evacuate these troops or Austria threatened to attack. William II supported Austria's demand and the Serbians withdrew. Thus although the Balkan countries had shown that they could settle their own affairs without involving the Great Powers in war, Austria

Greek Forces, 1912

and Serbia still faced each other in bitter hatred. Serbia did not believe it could ever become completely independent while the Austro-Hungarian Empire survived. Austria did not believe it could survive the growing threat of Pan-Slavism unless Serbia was crushed. Moreover, William II's support for Austria showed, as in 1908, a policy towards the Balkans completely the opposite to that of Bismarck.

By 1913 William, like many people in Europe, did not believe that the great powers could remain permanently at peace. He began to speak of the 'approaching war', 'the fight to finish between Germans and Slavs'. 'It is bound to come', he wrote in May 1913. 'When? We shall soon see.' William told his Foreign Office to make military agreements with Bulgaria, Turkey and Romania. 'This is Germany's "to be or not to be"', he wrote.

One obvious result of this growing feeling that war was inevitable was that the great powers began spending much more on armaments. This had already been happening for several years in Britain and Germany with naval spending. After the 1908 Balkan crisis, Russia began to modernize and expand its army. In December 1913 the Tsar decided to increase the peacetime strength by half a million. France also increased the length of compulsory service in 1913. In Britain, between 1907 and 1912, Lord Haldane had created the Territorial Army as a trained reserve to supplement the small Regular Army. Germany also took steps to increase its army. A bill passed by the Reichstag early in 1913 planned a growth from 663,000 men to 761,000 with a further 40,000 by 1914. This growth of armies created fear and made it more likely that a nation would strike at the moment when it felt itself strongest. This policy had been suggested several years earlier in Britain when Germany was building up its fleet.

Sarajevo and Beyond

Early in June 1914 William travelled to Austria to visit the Archduke Franz-Ferdinand, heir to the throne. The weather was glorious and William was always sure of a friendly welcome from Germany's oldest ally. Franz-Ferdinand was more liberal than most in Austria. He did not support the call for war with Serbia. He believed that the Empire of Austria and Hungary should become the Empire of Austrians, Hungarians *and* Slavs to prevent a complete break-up. Franz-Ferdinand told William of his coming visit to Sarajevo, the capital of Bosnia, to attend Army manœuvres. William returned to Berlin on 16 June and shortly afterwards left for the naval Regatta at Kiel. On Sunday, 28 June he was at sea in his racing yacht *Meteor* when a motor launch approached bearing Admiral Muller, Chief of the Naval Cabinet. Muller told William that Archduke Franz-Ferdinand and his wife Elisabeth had been attacked while driving through Sarajevo. Both had died of gunshot wounds.

William was horrified by 'the cowardly detestable crime'. He remembered bitterly the happy meeting a few days before when he had talked with Franz-Ferdinand and his family. Most of all it was the murder of an heir to an imperial throne which appalled William. To him this killing of royalty was an unpardonable crime. Nevertheless, he did not go to the funeral, having been warned of a plot to kill him next.

The Austrian government was unsure how to react to the murder. Some, supported by the generals, demanded an immediate invasion; others wanted to wait. Nothing could be done until the attitude of Berlin was known. Accordingly Emperor Francis-Joseph II sent a letter to William II blaming not only Serbian terrorists for the murder but the Serbian Government as well. 'As Serbia is the centre of Pan-Slavism', he concluded, 'it must be eliminated as a political factor in the Balkans.'

Both William and his Chancellor agreed that Serbia must be punished even at the risk of provoking Russia to war. It was Austria's task to deal with Serbia as she saw fit, but 'whatever Austria's decision may be, Austria can count with certainty upon it that Germany will stand by her friend and ally'. William and his government were convinced, or perhaps hoped desperately, that Russia and France would remain neutral while Serbia was crushed. The German government persuaded William to leave for his annual cruise off Norway on 6 July.

Encouraged by German support the Austrian government decided to punish Serbia. On 23 July a note was sent to Belgrade containing terms so harsh that, it was thought in Vienna, Serbia would be certain to refuse. This would then provide the excuse to declare war. Surprisingly Serbia accepted the terms, but encouraged by hints of Russian support, made one or two conditions. The German government meanwhile was trying to persuade the other powers that an Austro-Serbian war need involve no one else. On 27 July William returned in haste from Norway and urged Austria to accept Serbia's terms. It was too late. Encouraged by German statesmen and generals and by its own General Staff, Austria declared war on Serbia on the 28th. The following day Belgrade, the Serbian capital, was bombarded.

Russia did not stand by as she had done in 1908 but began mobilising her army. Germany, threatened by an invasion by Russia, also began rapid mobilization and, according to long-prepared plans, called on Austria to face Russia while the German army dealt with the French. Firstly the Germans called on Russia to halt mobilization. Russia refused and on 1 August Germany declared war. This automatically brought the Franco-Russian alliance into action. Although it was thought possible that Britain might stay out if France was not attacked, Germany had only one plan prepared – a hammer-blow against France followed by a longer campaign against Russia. On 3 August, Germany declared war on France and the following day began the attack through neutral Belgium. At this point Britain made her position clear. Under the terms of a treaty of 1839 Britain was a protector of Belgium. Germany was given twelve hours notice to withdraw but failed to do so. At midnight on 4 August Britain and Germany were at war.

'To think that George and Nicky have played me false,' said William. 'If my grandmother had been alive, she would never have allowed it.'

11 Commander-in-Chief

The Army

On 4 August 1914 the German invasion through Belgium began, designed to overwhelm France in a few weeks. As Supreme Commander of the German armed forces William felt it was his duty to be with his troops. On 16 August he duly left Berlin in the royal train, freshly painted green, and made his way to army headquarters at Koblenz on the Rhine. The generals, who already had a poor opinion of William as a leader of armies, soon found his presence a nuisance. For more than twenty years William had lived in fear of finding Germany, without an ally of real value, fighting a two-front war against a European alliance. In 1914 this nightmare became reality. He became pale and haggard, looking ten years older in the first weeks of war.

The first crisis to test William's powers of leadership came almost at once, when Russian troops invaded East Prussia. The arrival of foreign troops on German soil was deeply insulting to William. The army commander, General Moltke, understanding William's feelings, ordered troops to be moved from the Western front to the Eastern. Moltke acted against the advice of the other generals, and even before the troops from the West could arrive, the Russians had been heavily defeated. Meanwhile the German advance in the West had been weakened. It was also threatened by a heavy attack from the British Expeditionary Force. Moltke lost his nerve; so did William, and the German retreat from the Paris road began.

This crisis of leadership destroyed the last shreds of William's self-confidence. He was unable to concentrate for more than a few moments at even the most important meetings. The General Staff almost completely ignored him. Yet William continued to behave outwardly like a commander. He talked eagerly about German victories and 'piles of enemy corpses, two metres high'. At the same time he worried deeply about the new forms of warfare – submarine attacks, and bombing. William continued to live at army headquarters, steaming back and forth between the Eastern and Western fronts.

William with four of his sons, 1916 (note his left arm)

He spent his time inspecting parades, decorating heroes and entertaining foreign guests. Thus as the war progressed William lived an increasingly remote and unreal existence. He played no part in directing the armies and endured none of the hardships of the front-line troops. By staying away from Berlin and other industrial centres, he did little to encourage and unite his people.

Meanwhile the failure to break through on the Western front in 1914 had led to a change of strategy. During 1915 the German army launched heavy attacks against the Russians while the British and French were allowed to batter in vain against Germany's western defences. In spite of forcing the Russians back over wide areas of Galicia and Poland, victory was as far off by the end of 1915 as it has been a year previously.

The Navy

Although William realized that he had lost all control over the army he was determined not to lose the navy, his own creation, in the same way. He quickly let both Tirpitz and Admiral Pöhl, the Chief of Naval Staff, know that only he, the Kaiser, could issue orders for the fleet to sail. At the outbreak of war, William quickly ordered all ships to return to base; of those in distant waters, all were driven from the seas by March 1915. William hoped that the British would come within range of his ships and they could then be dealt with singly or in small groups until their superiority was lost.

138

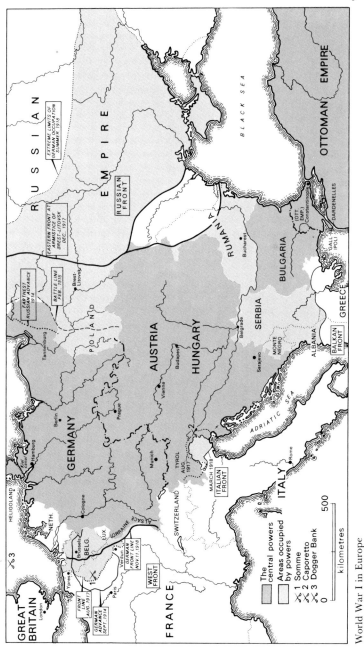

World War I in Europe

William was surprised that the British fleet, apart from one quick raid into the Heligoland Bight, stayed clear of German waters. Instead Britain imposed a blockade, preventing any ships, enemy or neutral, from reaching German ports. By heavy patrolling in the Channel and the North Sea Britain was able to stop completely most of Germany's seaborne trade. Over the following two to three years the blockade became a stranglehold on German living standards and industrial production.

As the first winter approached William recovered some of his confidence in naval matters and allowed small squadrons to cross the North Sea to lay mines and bombard English coastal towns. However, in January 1915 a raiding force was surprised by a British squadron off Dogger Bank and suffered serious casualties. William immediately ordered an end to the raids.

Admiral Tirpitz wanted a full-scale battle with the British in the North Sea as soon as possible. Although Britain had a superiority of 24 to 16 in Dreadnoughts it was unlikely that she would have been able to use them all in one battle. It was, moreover, generally known that Britain was building new Dreadnoughts so fast that soon she would have twice as many as Germany. What was not immediately obvious, fortunately for Britain, was the higher standard of German gunnery and armour-plating. William was utterly opposed to risking the loss of his beloved fleet. In the early stages he believed that a land victory over France and Russia would lead to bargaining with Britain. An intact fleet would then strengthen William's hand.

Unable to bring about a battle of the fleets Tirpitz pressed William to use submarines. The German navy possessed only twenty-nine of these in 1914 and fifty-four by 1916. In spite of this and at the risk of angering the USA, Germany announced in February 1915 that all enemy merchant vessels found near Britain would be sunk and the safety of neutrals could not be guaranteed. This policy led to the sinking of the *Lusitania* in May 1915 with the loss of 139 American lives. Fearful of America joining the war William halted the U-boat campaign for the time being. Tirpitz disagreed and wanted to resign but William would not allow him to. Nevertheless something had to be done to break the British blockade. Once again the German navy began making sallies into the North Sea, this time with William's reluctant approval. Inevitably a major clash occurred (Jutland,

May 1916). British losses were heavy, causing William to exclaim, 'the first mighty hammer-stroke has fallen, the spell of Trafalgar has been broken'. Once again William became terrified at the prospect of losing his fleet and he gave orders that there was not to be a repeat performance. For the rest of the war the German fleet lay at anchor.

The Home Front

The British blockade was made more effective by the lack of preparation in Germany for a long war. Before the war Germany produced about 80 per cent of its own food and it could still get milk, eggs and meat from Scandinavia, Holland and the Balkans. In 1914 large numbers of farm workers went to join the army. Horses and oxen were taken away for Army transport. There was a serious shortage of chemical fertilizers since the ingredients were needed to make explosives. In addition the weather was bad. The grain harvest of 1917 produced only half the 1913 total, and the potato crops of 1916–18 were very low. Bread rationing was introduced in January 1915 soon to be followed by all foodstuffs. The winter of 1916–17 was known as the 'turnip winter' because there was little else to eat. Most people got only 60 per cent of the food needed to remain healthy. Clothing was in short supply. Miners joined the armed forces. This caused a coal shortage and the extra misery of cold and burst pipes. William rarely visited the great cities so he could have little idea of what the civilian population was suffering.

German industry, like that in Britain, had no plans to change over to full-scale war production. Vital workers drifted into the army. The Royal Navy prevented Germany shipping exports. This created unemployment so that industry was not fully geared to the war effort until April 1915. However, in the control of important raw materials the State took command as early as 8 August 1914. Walter Rathenau, head of AEG, the huge electrical firm, organized this aspect of the German war effort. Scientists worked to find substitute material such as synthetic rubber. The extraction of nitrogen from the air was the most important development.

Because of the shortage of adult male workers there was large-scale recruiting of women and boys into industry. By 1917 nearly 40 per cent of the Krupps labour force were women. Long hours, including Sundays, were worked. In December 1916 all males from seventeen to sixty were obliged by law to work for the war economy. In the early days of the war Germany's soldiers and workers happily put up with sacrifice and hardships. By the middle of 1916 the Russians were advancing again. On the Western front the terrible blood-lettings at Verdun and the Somme increased Germany's total of dead and wounded to over 2·5 million. The possibility of a German victory had vanished from most people's minds. Many began to look coldly and critically at those who ruled the Empire.

America

William was no less depressed than his subjects by the lack of a real victory, though for different reasons. He could feel only inevitable defeat and his own fall. In one sense William's fall had already begun.

After the military failures of 1916 General Hindenburg was appointed Chief of the General Staff, with General Ludendorff as his right-hand man. The two became virtually military dictators of Germany. William became even more of a shadow among the rulers of Germany. The basic problem, which seemed impossible to solve, was that to win the war Germany

General von Hindenburg

had to win in the West. There the 400-mile front was so heavily defended that every small gain cost thousands of casualties. In the East bigger advances and victories were possible but the capture of huge areas of Russian territory would not win the war.

When he learnt that Chancellor Bethmann and the Foreign Office had been putting out peace feelers, William, not surprisingly, encouraged them. Ludendorff especially was opposed to anything short of total victory. However, on 6 December 1916 Germany defeated Romania and with the confidence of a victor sent a note to the *Entente* powers. Lloyd George, the new British Prime Minister, made a similar approach to Ludendorff. Then President Woodrow Wilson of America intervened. On 18 December he called on the powers to state their war and peace aims so that a peace plan might be found. The *Entente* demanded that Belgium, Serbia, Alsace-Lorraine, Poland and other German-occupied territories should be handed back; freedom for the subject peoples of Austria-Hungary, which meant the end of that empire; and the expulsion of Turkey from Europe.

The Americans regarded the *Entente* demands as impossible. Had Germany at that moment put forward moderate suggestions it is possible that the USA might have backed them and even threatened to cut off supplies to Britain and France to get peace. Unfortunately, Wilson was regarded in Germany as being 'pro-British'. Hindenburg, Ludendorff and their followers were not prepared to have a peace unless Germany at least kept Belgium and large territories in eastern Europe.

On 31 January 1917 German peace proposals were handed to Wilson. The Germans also told Wilson that unrestricted submarine attacks would begin again the following day. Wilson immediately broke off diplomatic relations with Germany. Less than three months later the USA declared war on Germany.

The decision to restart submarine attacks had been taken in the New Year of 1917. Germany was in the grip of near-starvation. The military position seemed hopeless and the USA was known to have only a small army. The generals urged that Britain would be defeated within six months, by submarines. Bethmann and some ministers argued that a German victory was by no means certain but a United States declaration of war would be. William, probably against his better judgment, sided with the generals. In July 1917 the first American troops landed in France.

Russia

Germany then not only missed the opportunity of a reasonable peace in the New Year 1917, but unwittingly threw away possible victory by resuming submarine warfare so quickly. For in the early months of 1917 massive Anglo-French attacks slithered to a halt in a sea of mud and mutiny broke out in the French army. Even more important, revolution broke out in Russia. The sufferings of Nicholas II's subjects had been even greater than those of William's. A bread riot in Petrograd was sufficient to start the train of events leading to the Bolshevik takeover. To bring about more turmoil and the possible withdrawal of Russia from the war, the German High Command allowed Lenin, the Bolshevik leader, to pass through Germany in a sealed train on his way from Switzerland to Russia. Thus by the spring of 1917, both France and Russia were showing severe strain from nearly three years' fighting. Additionally if Russia's raw materials could have been tapped Germany might still have beaten the blockade. Instead Germany now faced increasing numbers of American troops in France. Meanwhile the US navy, then the third largest in the world, was playing its part in the Atlantic. Combined with the British convoy system the submarine attacks, as Bethmann had prophesied, were being beaten off.

To add to the general gloom Austria-Hungary, now under the new Emperor, Charles, warned Germany that it could not survive another winter of war. In Germany, following the 'turnip winter' there was a growing wish for peace. The Centre Party sided with the Socialists in demanding a peace without annexations. Infuriated by the 'Reichstag revolt', Hindenburg and Ludendorff informed William that unless Chancellor Bethmann was replaced they would resign. The two generals were thus using a power which was the Emperor's alone. Nevertheless, glad to rid himself of further responsibilities, William agreed. Bethmann resigned in July 1917 and George Michaelis, Prussian Minister of Agriculture, was appointed by the military 'government'. As the spokesman of the military Michaelis was unable to win the support of the Reichstag and after three months he resigned. His successor, a half-blind Bavarian, Count Hertling, was more popular with the political parties and this suited the generals, who were busy planning the 1918 offensives.

By the end of 1917 the military situation was again turning in Germany's favour, if the steady build-up of American troops could be ignored. In October the Italians were heavily defeated at Caporetto. In November the Bolsheviks seized power and within hours were broadcasting appeals for an armistice. This was granted and German divisions began pulling out from the

Russo–German peace talks delegates, 1917

Russian front heading for France. Peace terms were less easy to agree on. Only the threat of a German occupation of Moscow and Petrograd persuaded the Bolsheviks to agree to Germany's harsh demands for Russian territories. Lenin was convinced that Germany also would be overtaken by revolution and the territories would be handed back. William played no part in the negotiations with the Bolsheviks. He believed that if Germany increased the number of foreign subjects through annexations it would create future troubles. When William tried to put these views forward, Hindenburg and Ludendorff again simply offered their resignations.

The annexations proved a failure. The High Command left a million men in Russia to try to extract food and raw materials. Only 42,000 wagon loads of corn actually arrived in Germany.

Defeat

Meanwhile the other million troops from the Eastern front had joined up with the armies of the Western front for Germany's final bid for victory. Supreme Headquarters was moved to Spa in Belgium. William moved into a nearby house. The offensive began on 21 March 1918 and made rapid progress. At St Quentin 90,000 British troops and 2 million bottles of whisky were captured. 'The battle is won, the English have been utterly defeated', cried William. Then the attack began to slow up through exhaustion and heavy losses. The second and third offensives in April and May followed similar patterns.

The last German offensive began on 15 July but faltered in less than a week when the Americans and French counter-attacked. On 8 August British and Commonwealth troops supported by tanks broke through the German lines. The German High Command abandoned all hope of victory; the Allied armies continued to press forward. On 29 September Ludendorff demanded a cease-fire if an invasion of Germany was to be prevented.

Abdication

William left army headquarters in August and went to his castle at Wilhelmshöhe. The Empress had suffered a heart attack and William decided his duty was to look after his wife. By the end of September the politicians were demanding that he return to Spa to deal with the military and political crisis. As a necessary preliminary to seeking an armistice a new government had been formed representing all parties, including the Socialists. It was led by Prince Max of Baden, a liberal nobleman. Military defeat gave Germany its first genuine parliamentary government. On 3 October Prince Max wrote to President Wilson asking for peace. Wilson's reply and a later note demanded German withdrawal from enemy territory, the end of submarine attacks and the dismissal of Germany's 'undemocratic rulers'. On the 24th Wilson spelt out his message clearly. Unless the Kaiser and the General Staff were deposed, the USA would seek not peace talks but the surrender of Germany. Ludendorff had by now recovered his nerve and hotly opposed Wilson's demands. Prince Max went to William and told him to choose between the government and Ludendorff.

William chose and Ludendorff fled to Sweden in disguise. It was now clear that as long as William remained Kaiser and King of Prussia he was an obstacle to peace. Evidently it was not clear to William for he set out for Spa once more where he felt safe amongst the generals. Somehow Max had to make William realize the seriousness of the situation for a mutiny had broken out in the German navy and was rapidly becoming a revolution, spreading across the country.

The Socialists, who found themselves struggling with the Communists for control of the revolution, were willing to keep the monarchy. They were not willing to support William, however, but wanted his eldest grandson to succeed. William's reaction to the revolution was to discuss plans to lead the army against the rebels. The generals realized that the exhausted army would side with the revolutionaries, as had happened in Russia. 'Sire,' General Gröner told William, 'you no longer have an army.' At last William began to realize his position but even so clung to the hope that he might remain King of Prussia.

Meanwhile in Berlin vast demonstrations were taking place. Civil war would break out unless William went. Frantic telephone messages passed from Berlin to Spa. William's delay in fact brought about the collapse of the monarchy. In Berlin the Communists seized the Imperial Palace and declared Germany to be a Soviet Republic. In panic the Socialists quickly declared Germany to be a Socialist Republic (*below*). On 9 November 1918 William's reign as Emperor of Germany came to an end.

Declaration of the German Republic

12 The Squire of Doorn

Exile

The immediate problem arose of what to do with William now that he was no longer the Kaiser. The roads to the front line and to Berlin were held by revolutionary troops. At all costs the generals wanted to save William from the fate of Nicholas II, shot by the Bolsheviks in July 1918. The only route still open was northwards to neutral Holland, where William might be safe from both the extreme German revolutionaries and the British and French who were already baying for his blood.

It took William nearly five hours to make up his mind. He almost considered remaining in Germany when he heard that the Empress, Dona, was unharmed in Berlin. Before dawn on 10 November he left Spa in a motor convoy and crossed the Dutch border at Eysen. News of his arrival was telephoned to The Hague and William and his followers had to sit for six hours in a waiting-room whilst the Dutch government decided. A special train was then sent to collect the German party and the next day William was met by Dutch officials and the German Ambassador. 'I am a broken man,' William told the Ambassador, 'how can I begin life again? My prospects are hopeless. I have nothing left to believe in.' He was then told that a Count Bentinck had offered to put his house at Amerongen at William's disposal. As they drove into the grounds later that day William turned to his host and said 'now for a good cup of English tea'. On the same day, 11 November, Europe was enjoying its first moments of peace for more than four years; a peace which had cost 10 million lives.

William lived at Amerongen until the spring of 1920. The house, which was fortunately moated and fortified, was besieged by journalists and sightseers from all over the world. The Empress arrived at Amerongen a fortnight after William, having suffered no ill-treatment or hardship at the hands of the revolutionaries in Berlin. She was still suffering from heart trouble and worried terribly about William's safety for the British government hoped to put the ex-Kaiser on trial. Sometimes she awoke crying, 'They're coming for him.' As the months went by William's band of followers gradually took their leave and returned to Germany until only four officers were left. Captain Iselmann, the youngest, married Count Bentinck's daughter and remained with William until his death. Meanwhile William lived quietly. He attended family prayers each morning, chopped wood for exercise, read *The Times* and books in English, and talked politics until the early hours of the morning. He completely shunned active politics, a promise he had made to the Dutch.

The World War concluded with the Treaty of Versailles, signed in June 1919. Article 27 accused the German Emperor of 'a supreme offence against international morality and the sanctity of Treaties'. Some 830 Germans were named as 'war criminals', including Bethmann and Hindenburg. On 10 January 1920 the Dutch government was asked to hand William over for trial but this it adamantly refused to do. The Allied governments then let the matter drop.

Doorn

Several weeks after the unsuccessful attempt to have him brought to trial, William bought Doorn House. Originally built as a fortified manor house in the fourteenth century and largely rebuilt in the eighteenth, Doorn House stood in extensive grounds, about 7 kilometres from Amerongen. The German government allowed William to remove his furniture, books, pictures and household goods from the royal palaces in Berlin and Potsdam. A large guest house was built near the gates for the numerous visitors. In this peaceful spot William spent the remaining twenty-one years of his life.

Dona, his wife, was unhappy with life in Holland. Her health was poor and she missed the company of her daughter, now Duchess of Brunswick. The Empress's sons unknowingly had added to her unhappiness. Prince Eitel Frederick's marriage had long since broken up; Prince Joachim was a rake who committed suicide in 1920; Crown Prince William had, against the wishes of both his father and the General Staff, also fled to Holland in 1918 and was considered to have dishonoured the royal name. In February 1921 William and Dona celebrated their fortieth wedding anniversary. Two months later, on

11 April, she died. With his five remaining sons, all in uniform, William watched her coffin placed on a special train to Berlin. Neither the ex-Kaiser nor the ex-Crown Prince were allowed to travel on the train to Germany. This was probably for the best since William was almost collapsing with grief. The other four sons went on for the funeral service at Potsdam. For many weeks afterwards William was deeply distressed. He had Dona's room left exactly as it was with the door locked.

A year after Dona's death William received a letter of loyalty from a little German boy. He was so impressed that he invited the boy and his widowed mother, Princess Hermine, to visit him at Doorn. Within a week William and Hermine became engaged and the wedding took place on 5 November 1922. Hermine, twenty-eight years younger than William, was believed to have plotted the letter, the meeting and the marriage. Nevertheless, she gave new life to William and his happiness was obvious for all to see.

Life at Doorn passed pleasantly enough. William still read English newspapers and books as well as German ones. He

The interior of Doorn House

received many letters which he faithfully answered. Wood-chopping remained his favourite exercise but he also cultivated trees and roses. He enjoyed a sleep after lunch since he was kept busy entertaining house guests, members of his family and leading men from many countries. He talked politics, but true to his promise, never made public speeches. He did, however, find time to write at length, with the help of a German journalist, Rosen. In 1922 he published *My Memoirs* in which he naturally tried to reduce his own responsibility for the war, which had been laid upon him so heavily. This was followed by *My Early Life* in 1923 and *Memories of Corfu* in 1924. Four years later the letters from his mother to Queen Victoria were published and in the German edition he wrote a preface. In 1929 he published a book about his Prussian ancestors. Archaeology had always been one of William's great interests and in 1933 the Doorn Research Community was formed to discuss this subject. One of the subjects discussed in 1934 and 1936 was the origin of the ancient Hindu symbol which by then hung everywhere in Germany – the swastika.

The Nazis

It would have been very surprising if William had, after thirty years as Emperor, abandoned all hope of ever regaining his throne. In 1930 the German Republic was, like much of the world, sliding into a terrible economic depression. Unemployment soared and the extreme National Socialist Party (Nazis) led by Adolf Hitler was thriving upon this misery. From twelve seats in 1928 the Nazis increased their numbers in the Reichstag to 132 in 1930. The Centrist Chancellor, Brüning, believed that one sure way to keep Hitler out of power would be to restore the monarchy. He knew that the moderate parties would never accept the ex-Kaiser or the ex-Crown Prince, but that they would accept William II's grandson Prince William of Prussia. Old Field-Marshal Hindenburg, who had been President of the Republic since 1925, refused to agree to the idea unless William II was brought back. Hindenburg had long regretted his disloyalty to William at Spa in November 1918 and he would allow no other king now. William, believing that he might still regain the throne under Hitler, was unwilling to throw away his claim by agreeing to his grandson being chosen.

Listening to Nazi propaganda in 1931–2, praising the Hohenzollern family, William felt he had good cause to wait. In 1932 one of Hitler's deputies, Hermann Göring, visited Doorn and told William that it was their dearest wish to restore the monarchy. William believed that the Nazis would revive German power and he allowed two of his sons to join the party. In January 1933 Hitler became Chancellor and the situation changed. William was allowed to draw an income from Germany only if he promised not to criticize the Nazi government. In January 1934 a celebration in Berlin to mark the ex-Kaiser's seventy-fifth birthday was broken up by the police. A year later William asked the ex-Crown Prince to get Hitler's permission for him (William II) to return to Germany. Hitler absolutely refused to allow it.

The Last Years

After 1935 William was naturally bitter towards Hitler, not only because he had been deceived, but also because, like so many others, he was slow to realize the essential evils of Nazism. William was horrified by the treatment of the Jews and other minority groups by the Nazi storm-troopers. As a religious man he also heard of the Nazi attacks on the Christian Churches with disgust. He watched sorrowfully as Europe began to slide once more towards war.

By contrast William felt a growing affection for Britain. He read even more English books and papers, welcomed visitors from Britain and was fascinated by the Coronation of King George VI in 1937. When Neville Chamberlain, the British Prime Minister, flew to Germany in September 1938 to try to prevent a German invasion of Czechoslovakia, William was full of praise for him. In Britain the former 'war criminal' began to appear as an angel of peace, by comparison with the threat of Hitlerism. The British government even began to worry about his safety if Hitler ordered a German invasion of Holland.

In May 1940 the German invasion of Holland duly took place. Winston Churchill, the new British Prime Minister, and King George VI agreed to offer William refuge in Britain. A message was sent via the British ambassador to the Mayor of Utrecht who personally delivered it to William. The latter was very pleased to receive it but he did not wish to run away again as he had in November 1918. 'Old trees cannot be transplanted,' he said.

Hitler issued strict orders that the German army was to keep well away from Doorn House but curiosity was too strong. Eventually the *Gestapo* put a guard on the house. William used to walk to the gates for a chat with the guards but he also talked to many officers who were smuggled in through the back door. In June 1940 William made his last public gesture when he sent a telegram to Hitler congratulating him on the capture of Paris.

A year later William fell ill with stomach trouble. He then developed a blood clot on the lung and became unconscious. At 11.30 a.m. on 4 June 1941 he died, in the presence of his wife and daughter, at the age of eighty-two. By contrast with his grandfather William I, who received several pages of notice in *The Times* in 1888, William II's obituary covered only three columns. In German papers he received one column at the bottom of the front page.

Princess Hermine, his second wife, died in 1947, a prisoner of the Russian army. His four eldest sons all died between 1942 and 1951.

William and Princess Hermine

Epilogue – May–June 1941

A few weeks before William's death, the most heavily armoured battleship in the world, built in Germany in 1940, sailed into the North Sea. It weighed 45,000 tons and carried eight 34-cm guns. Barring its way were the British battleship *Prince of Wales* and the old battle cruiser *Hood*. The latter sank at the fifth salvo and the armoured monster passed into the Atlantic, hunted by the whole British Home Fleet. For if it were not quickly found and sunk it would have begun destroying the merchant convoys from America. On the 26 May 1941 a Catalina flying-boat spotted the German battleship heading for the port of Brest in occupied France. Aircraft from the carrier *Ark Royal* dived into the attack with aerial torpedoes damaging its propeller and jamming the rudder. Finally after a tremendous pounding from the guns of the British fleet the German battleship sank. Its name was the *Bismarck*.

This greatest of German monuments to the famous statesman was not the only memory of Bismarck which disappeared at this time. Less than three weeks after William's death at Doorn, Germany for the second time in thirty years took a step which Bismarck had always regarded as probable suicide – war with Russia. In 1914–17, thanks to unhappy conditions in Russia, Germany had emerged victorious. In 1922, 1926 and 1939, the two countries had signed treaties, but Adolf Hitler wanted all the vast lands and wealth of European Russia. On 22 June 1941 over three million troops from Germany and its allies attacked the Soviet Union. Great changes had taken place in Russia since 1917; the country was much stronger and the people were prepared to fight and die far more willingly than they had been for the Tsar. At great cost and bloodshed Russia stopped the German attack and hurled it back. In May 1945 the Russian army captured Berlin and Germany was broken in two between East and West.

Thus in the early summer of 1941 there disappeared not only the symbols of Imperial Germany but ultimately what

Bismarck and William II had struggled to create and preserve; a strong, respected and united Germany.

Among Germany's former enemies it has been common to see a natural and evil succession through that country's leaders – Bismarck, William II, Hitler. The first was the conqueror of Central Europe; the second, the would-be conqueror of the continent, and the third, the would-be conqueror of the world. These three leaders had some notable similarities of character. Bismarck and William were both devout protestants, ardent monarchists and, like Hitler, anti-democratic. Bismarck and Hitler were merciless in war, hungry for power and without pity for those who crossed them. William II and Hitler were both great talkers and speechmakers and loved flattery but lacked the ability to concentrate. When these points have been noticed, the argument for a 'line of succession' appears to be mainly unfounded.

Bismarck was without doubt the outstanding world statesman of the nineteenth century. 'When he came to power in 1862, Germany was a confederation of independent states fossilized in the mould of 1815; when he left office Germany was a united nation, a state of great stature, feared and respected by the Great Powers.'[1] His ambitions for conquest were limited so for twenty years he successfully kept the peace. The system he had created survived in part for another quarter-century. Although his motives were doubtful, Bismarck created a welfare system which has become the model for the world. His major failure was his inability to understand the changes taking place around him. He thought in terms of the eighteenth century; the privileged few who ruled and the mass of serfs who worked. He had no understanding of the hopes and ideals of industrial workers, of the development of parliamentary rule in many parts of Europe and the lessening powers of kings and emperors. Bismarck prevented parliamentary development in Germany, a policy which William and his ministers tried less successfully to continue. Thus Germany did not gain the opportunity to practise genuine parliamentary rule until 1918. At this time political and economic difficulties prevented its succeeding.

William II was not satisfied with the frontiers of 1871 as Bismarck had been. This is understandable for by 1900 the age

[1] Carr, *A History of Germany 1815–1945*, p. 165.

of continental powers had begun; the USA; Russia reaching to the Pacific; the expanding empire of Japan and the world-wide power and possessions of Britain and France. For Britain certainly, then ruling almost a quarter of the world, it would have been very acceptable if frontier changes could have been frozen for ever. To guard these possessions Britain felt she needed a 'two power' navy which gave her the means but not the right to rule the seas. William may have unwisely threatened Britain with his navy but he had every right to build one. If Germany wished to join the ranks of world powers then a big navy, in 1900, was vital. This did not mean that William intended to use the navy in anger; indeed when the time came he did his best to immobilize it. The navy was for William's personal glory, though Britain could scarcely be expected to realize this.

Although 1914–18 has been popularly called the 'Kaiser's War' there is no real truth in this title. William did not mind a war in south-eastern Europe, but the last thing he wanted was the full-scale continental war which broke out. Once he and his ministers had committed themselves to supporting Austria in July 1914 there was, unfortunately, no turning back. It should have been clear to them that Germany and her allies could not possibly defeat Britain, France and Russia, particularly with the shadows of America and Japan in the background.

William himself was too weak to be able either to understand or to change what was happening between 1900–14 both in Germany and in Europe. He was unable to hold back those with big ambitions in the Foreign Office or on the General Staff. He obstructed those who were trying to keep to a more reasonable path. William simply was not big enough for his role in life.

Bismarck then was a man with a definite aim in life which, once achieved, he took care not to lose. William's ambitions were vaguer but he had neither the personality nor the means to achieve them; nor could he control the events which carried him along. 'It was not his fault,' wrote Winston Churchill. 'It was his fate.'

Biographical Notes

AEHRENTHAL, Alois, Count von (1854–1912). Austrian politician. Ambassador to Romania 1895 and to Russia 1899. Foreign Minister 1906–11.

BETHMANN-HOLLWEG, Theobald von (1856–1921). German politician. Civil servant in Prussia. State Secretary for the interior 1907–9. Chancellor 1909–1917.

BULOW, Bernhard, Prince von (1849–1929). German politician. Diplomatic Service 1874. Ambassador to Rome 1893–7 and 1914–15. Foreign Secretary 1897–1900. Chancellor 1900–09.

CAPRIVI, Georg Leo, Count von (1831–99). German general and politician. On General Staff 1883–8. Army Commander, Hannover 1888–90. Chancellor 1890–4.

DISRAELI, Benjamin (Lord Beaconsfield) (1804–81). British politician, M.P. 1837. Novelist. Chancellor of Exchequer 1852, 1858–9, 1867. Prime Minister 1868, 1874–80.

GORCHAKOV, Alexander, Prince (1798–1883). Russian politician. Ambassador to Vienna 1854. Foreign Minister 1856–82. Helped found Three Emperors League.

HINDENBURG, Paul von, Field-Marshal (1847–1934). German soldier and politician. Served in Austrian and French wars. Retired 1911. Recalled 1914. Chief of General Staff 1916–18. Retired 1919. President of German Republic 1925–34.

HOHENLÖHE-SCHILLINGSFURST, Chlodwig, Prince Zu (1819–1901). German politician. Bavarian Minister-President 1866–70. Ambassador to Paris, 1874. Governor, Alsace-Lorraine 1885. Chancellor 1894–1900.

HOLSTEIN, Friedrich, Baron von (1837–1919). German Foreign Office official of great influence 1878–1906.

ISVOLSKY, Alexander, Prince (1856–1919). Russian diplomat from 1875–1917. Tokyo 1899. Copenhagen 1903. Foreign Minister 1906–10. Ambassador to Paris 1910–17.

LENIN (Vladimir Ilyich Ulyanov) (1870–1924). Russian revolutionary politician. Exiled to Siberia 1897–1900. Western Europe 1900–17. Head of Soviet government 1917–24.

LLOYD GEORGE, David (1863–1945). British politician. Liberal M.P. 1890–1945. President, Board of Trade 1905. Chancellor of Exchequer 1908–15. Prime Minister 1916–22.

LUDENDORFF, Eric, Field Marshal (1865–1937). German soldier and would-be politician. Army 1882, Major-General 1914. Quartermaster-General 1916. Supported Hitler 1923–25.

SALISBURY, Marquess of (1830–1903). British politician. Conservative M.P. 1853; Secretary for India 1866, 1874–78; Foreign Secretary 1878–80, 1885–1892, 1895–1900; Prime Minister 1885–92, 1895–1902.

SHUVALOV, Pavel, Count (1830–1908). Russian diplomat. Ambassador to Germany 1885–94.

TIRPITZ, Alfred von, Admiral (1849–1930). German sailor and politician. Joined Navy 1865; torpedo specialist, Baltic Squadron. State Secretary for Navy 1897–1916. Reichstag 1924–28.

European Monarchs

Austria-Hungary	1797–1835 Francis II; 1835–48 Ferdinand; 1848–1916 Francis-Joseph II; 1916–18 Charles.
Britain	1820–30 George IV; 1830–37 William IV; 1837–1901 Victoria; 1901–10 Edward VII; 1910–35 George V
France	1815–24 Louis XVIII; 1824–30 Charles X; 1830–48 Louis-Philippe; 1848–52 Second Republic; 1852–70 Napoleon III; 1870–1940 Third Republic.
Germany (Prussia)	1797–1840 Frederick William III; 1840–61 Frederick William IV; 1861–88 William I; 1888 Frederick III; 1888–1918 William II.
Russia	1801–25 Alexander I; 1825–55 Nicholas I; 1855–81 Alexander II; 1881–94 Alexander III; 1894–1917 Nicholas II.

Economic Development

Germany and The Great Powers

POPULATION IN MILLIONS

	Germany	Britain	France	U.S.A.	Russia
1870	41	32	37	40	87
1890	49	38	38	63	111
1900	56	42	39	76	130
1913	67	46	40	95	174

COAL IN MILLIONS OF TONS

	Germany	Britain	France	U.S.A.	Russia
1870	38	118	13	37	1
1890	89	184	26	150	6
1900	149	228	33	244	16
1913	279	292	41	517	29

158

I STEEL IN MILLIONS OF TONS

	Germany	Britain	France	U.S.A.	Russia
1870	0·3	0·6	0·1	0·1	0·1
1890	2·2	3·6	0·7	4·3	0·4
1900	6·7	5·0	1·6	10·4	2·2
1913	18·9	7·8	4·7	31·8	3·6

⊞ RAILWAYS IN THOUSANDS OF KILOMETRES

	Germany	Britain	France	U.S.A.	Russia
1870	19	24	17	90	12
1890	43	33	36	250	30
1900	51	35	37	309	51
1910	61	38	50	384	70

% PERCENTAGE SHARE OF WORLD'S PRODUCTION

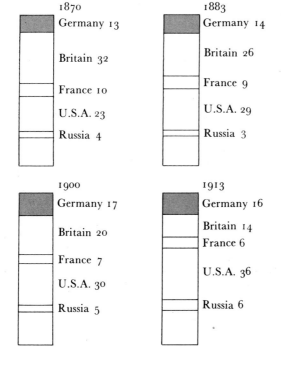

1870
Germany 13
Britain 32
France 10
U.S.A. 23
Russia 4

1883
Germany 14
Britain 26
France 9
U.S.A. 29
Russia 3

1900
Germany 17
Britain 20
France 7
U.S.A. 30
Russia 5

1913
Germany 16
Britain 14
France 6
U.S.A. 36
Russia 6

Family Tree of the Kaiser

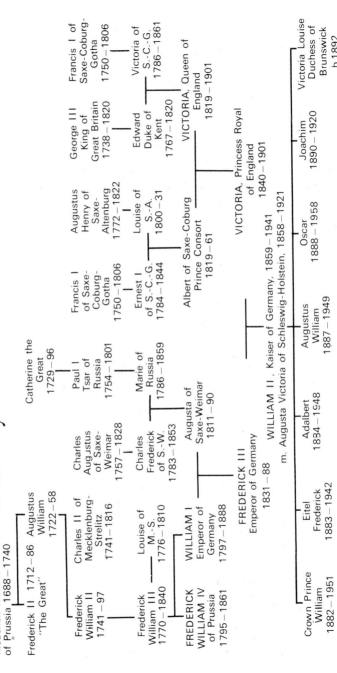

Further Reading

German history in the nineteenth and early twentieth centuries is well served by books in English. Bismarck himself has been the subject of many works; William II has been less well treated.

Background
W. CARR, *A History of Germany 1815–1945* (Edward Arnold 1969).
J. CLAPHAM, *Economic Development of France and Germany 1815–1914* (Cambridge University Press 1966)
W. H. DAWSON, *The German Empire 1867–1914*, 2 vols (Allen & Unwin 1967)
M. DILL, *Modern Germany: a history* (University of Michigan Press 1959)
H. HOLBORN, *A History of Modern Germany 1840–1945* (Eyre & Spottiswoode 1969)
G. MANN, *A History of Germany since 1789* (Chatto & Windus 1967)
E. J. PASSANT, *A Short History of Germany 1815–1945* (Cambridge University Press 1966)
K. S. PINSON, *Modern Germany,* 2nd edn (Collier-Macmillan 1967)
A. RAMM, *Germany 1789–1919* (Methuen 1967)

Bismarck
F. BAKER, *Bismarck* (Hutchinson Educational 1967)
BISMARCK, PRINCE OTTO VON, *His Reflections and Reminiscences* (Smith, Elder 1898)
E. EYCH, *Bismarck and the German Empire* (Allen & Unwin 1968)
J. HEADLAM, *Bismarck* (Putnam 1899)
W. JACKS, *Life of Prince Bismarck* (Collins 1899)
C. LOWE, *Prince Bismarck*, 2 vols (Cassell 1887)
W. RICHTER, *Bismarck* (Macdonald 1964)
C. G. ROBERTSON, *Bismarck* (Constable 1919)
L. SNYDER, *The Blood and Iron Chancellor* (Van Nostrand 1967)
A. J. P. TAYLOR, *Bismarck. The Man and the Statesman* (Hamish Hamilton 1955; New English Library 1968)

William II
T. AARONSON, *The Kaisers* (Cassell 1971)
M. BALFOUR, *The Kaiser and His Times* (Cresset Press 1964)
V. COWLES, *The Kaiser* (Collins 1963)
E. LUDWIG, *Kaiser William II* (Methuen 1927)
Adml. VON MULLER, *The Kaiser and His Court* (Macdonald 1963)
WILLIAM II, *Memoirs* (Cassell 1922)
WILLIAM II, *My Early Life* (Methuen 1923)

Index

Index